easy vegetarian one-pot

easy vegetarian one-pot

delicious fuss-free recipes for hearty meals

LONDON · NEW YORK

Designer Paul Stradling

Editor Rebecca Woods

Production Gordana Simakovic

Art Director Leslie Harrington

Publishing Director Alison Starling

Indexer Hilary Bird

First published in 2011
by Ryland Peters & Small
20–21 Jockey's Fields
London WC1R 4BW
and
Ryland Peters & Small, Inc.
519 Broadway, 5th Floor
New York, NY10012

www.rylandpeters.com

UK ISBN: 978 1 84975 159 9
10 9 8

US ISBN: 978 1 84975 160 5
10 9 8 7 6 5 4

Text © Nadia Arumugam, Ghillie Başan, Fiona
Beckett, Celia Brooks Brown, Maxine Clark,
Ross Dobson, Clare Ferguson, Silvana Franco,
Manisha Gambhir Harkins, Tonia George, Brian
Glover, Amanda Grant, Rachael Anne Hill, Annie
Nichols, Jane Noraika, Louise Pickford, Rena
Salaman, Jennie Shapter, Fiona Smith, Linda
Tubby, Sunil Vijayaker, Fran Warde, Laura
Washburn and Ryland Peters & Small 2011

Design and photographs
© Ryland Peters & Small 2011

A CIP record for this book is available from
the British Library.

US Library of Congress cataloging-in-publication
data has been applied for.

Printed in China

Notes

• All spoon measurements are level unless
otherwise specified.

• Weights and measurements have been
rounded up or down slightly to make
measuring easier.

• Eggs are medium unless otherwise
specified. Uncooked or partly cooked eggs
should not be served to the very young, the
very old, those with compromised immune
systems or to pregnant women.

• Where a frying pan/skillet size is specified,
this refers to the base measurement of the
pan, not the rim.

• Ovens should be preheated to the
specified temperature. Recipes in this book
were tested using a regular oven. If using a
fan-assisted oven, follow the manufacturer's
instructions for adjusting temperatures.

• When a recipe calls for the grated zest of
citrus fruit, buy unwaxed fruit and wash well
before using. If you can only find treated
fruit, scrub well in warm soapy water and
rinse before using.

• Cheeses started with animal rennet are
not suitable for vegetarians so read food
labelling careful and check that the cheese
you buy is made with a non-animal
(microbial) starter. Traditional Parmesan
is not vegetarian so we recommend a
vegetarian hard cheese (such as Gran
Moravia which has the same texture so
is ideal for grating) or Parma (a vegan
product). There is an increasing number of
manufacturers who are producing vegetarian
versions of traditionally non-vegetarian
cheeses, such as Gruyère or Gorgonzola.
Check online for suppliers in your location.

contents

introduction

Following a vegetarian diet is one of the simplest ways to ensure that you are adopting healthy eating habits – filling up on fresh vegetables and wholesome grains, beans and pulses/legumes, can help to ensure health and vitality.

But sometimes a busy life can mean that cooking can feel laborious rather than the pleasurable, stress-free activity it should be. Even the most enthusiastic of cooks will occasionally find, after a hard day at work, that it is far easier to reach for a ready-meal or dial for a pizza than to cook something wonderfully nourishing.

Whether you lack inspiration or energy, *Easy Vegetarian One-pot* will help by providing over 100 delicious, nutritious solutions for meals that require the minimum of fuss and preparation – all of which are suitable for those eating a vegetarian diet.

Divided into eight easy-to-navigate sections *Easy Vegetarian One-pot* covers a whole range of dishes – for every occasion and to suit every season – from lighter meals such as fresh crispy salads, or satisfying omelettes, which can be prepared in minutes on the stove-top, to hearty bakes and casseroles which can be left to cook slowly in the oven while you relax.

Drawing on exciting cuisines from around the world, the recipes are packed with flavour, guaranteed to delight, and show that eating delicious, healthy vegetarian food should never be a chore.

soups & salads

Puy lentils, grown in France, are great at thickening soups without turning sludgy. They give this soup a pert little bite which is offset by the soft, buttery vegetables and enriched by the heady tang of the dried oregano.

chunky puy lentil & vegetable soup

Melt the butter in a large casserole dish or heavy-based saucepan. Add the carrots, leeks, onion and garlic, and a large pinch of salt. Stir until everything is coated in butter and cook over medium heat, with the lid on, for 15 minutes, stirring occasionally.

Once the vegetables have softened, add the dried chilli/hot pepper flakes, oregano, tomatoes, lentils and stock. Cover again and leave to simmer for 30 minutes, or until the lentils are cooked. Season with salt and freshly ground pepper to taste.

Transfer to bowls and serve with buttered toast and grated cheese on the side.

50 g/4 tablespoons butter

2 carrots, peeled and finely chopped

2 leeks, white part only, thinly sliced

1 large onion, finely chopped

3 garlic cloves, sliced

½ teaspoon dried chilli/hot pepper flakes

2 teaspoons dried oregano

400-g/14-oz. can chopped plum tomatoes

200 g/7 oz. Puy lentils

1 litre/4 cups vegetable stock

sea salt and freshly ground black pepper

freshly grated Parmesan-style cheese (see note on page 4), to serve

crusty bread, toasted and buttered, to serve

serves 4–6

This is Lebanese in origin, but soups like this are served all over the Middle East. Crispy fried onions are a lovely topping, but you have to be brave and really brown them so they look almost black. In order to do this without burning them, you have to really soften them to start with.

lentil, spinach & cumin soup

3 tablespoons extra virgin olive oil

2 onions, sliced

4 garlic cloves, sliced

1 teaspoon ground coriander

1 teaspoon cumin seeds

150 g/5¼ oz. brown or green lentils

1.25 litres/5 cups vegetable stock

200 g/7 oz. spinach

freshly squeezed juice of 1 lemon

sea salt and freshly ground black pepper

to serve

4 tablespoons Greek yogurt

25 g/1 oz. pine nuts, lightly toasted

serves 4

Heat the olive oil in a large, heavy-based saucepan and add the onions. Cook, covered, for 8–10 minutes until softened. Remove half the onion and set aside.

Continue to cook the onion left in the pan for a further 10 minutes until deep brown, sweet, and caramelized. Take out and set aside to use for the garnish.

Return the softened onion to the pan and add the garlic, coriander, cumin seeds and lentils and stir for 1–2 minutes until well coated in oil. Add the stock, bring to the boil then turn down to a gentle simmer for 30 minutes until the lentils are lovely and soft.

Add the spinach and stir until wilted. Transfer half the soup to a blender and liquidize until you have a purée. Stir back into the soup. Season with lemon juice, sea salt and freshly ground black pepper.

Divide the soup between 4 bowls, add a dollop of Greek yogurt, and scatter the pine nuts and fried onions over the top.

Although minestrone is often thought of as cold weather fare, this version has summer written all over it and is packed with fresh tomatoes and green beans as well as chickpeas. And, as if it weren't already summery enough, a few handfuls of rocket/arugula add a peppery bite and the fresh taste lightens the soup, while making it much more than just another minestrone.

chickpea, tomato & green bean minestrone

Put the oil in a large saucepan set over medium heat. Add the onion, partially cover with a lid and cook for 4–5 minutes, stirring often, until softened. Add the garlic and cook for 1 minute. Add the green beans, chickpeas, tomatoes, parsley, stock and spaghetti and bring to the boil.

Reduce the heat and let simmer for 40 minutes, stirring often, until the pasta is cooked and the soup is thick. Season to taste with salt and pepper.

Just before serving, add the rocket/arugula and gently stir until the rocket/arugula softens. Ladle into warmed serving bowls and sprinkle a generous amount of grated pecorino over the top. Serve immediately with chunks of crusty bread.

Variation Try making this delicious soup with different vegetables. Courgettes/zucchini and carrots are a nice addition but remember that both take a little longer to cook so dice them very finely before adding to the soup with the other vegetables. A pinch of smoky Spanish paprika (pimentón) will add a slightly different flavour.

2 tablespoons olive oil

1 onion, chopped

2 garlic cloves, chopped

100 g/3½ oz. green beans, sliced on the angle

400-g/14-oz. can chickpeas, rinsed and drained

6 ripe tomatoes, halved

1 handful of chopped fresh flat leaf parsley

1.5 litres/6 cups vegetable stock

100 g/3½ oz. wholemeal/whole-wheat spaghetti, broken into pieces

50 g/2 oz. wild rocket/arugula leaves

50 g/2 oz. Parmesan-style cheese (see note on page 4), finely grated

sea salt and freshly ground black pepper

crusty bread, to serve

serves 4

A smaller, paler version of the borlotti bean, the pinto has an attractive orange-pink skin with rust-coloured specks. It's used extensively in Mexican cuisine, most familiarly in frijoles refritos (refried beans). Earthy and savoury in flavour, the beans go well with tomatoes, peppers and coriander/cilantro – pretty much all the best-loved flavours of the Americas.

100 g/3½ oz. dried pinto beans

2 tablespoons butter

1 tablespoon olive oil

1 red onion, chopped

2 garlic cloves, chopped

1 red bell pepper, deseeded and diced

2 carrots, chopped

2 teaspoons chilli powder

2 teaspoons ground cumin

2 bay leaves

1.5 litres/6 cups vegetable stock

400-g/14-oz. can chopped tomatoes

sea salt

to serve

1 small iceberg lettuce, finely shredded

sour cream

leaves from a small bunch of fresh coriander/cilantro

lime wedges

serves 4

spicy pinto bean soup with shredded lettuce & sour cream

Soak the beans in cold water overnight. Drain and set aside.

Heat the butter and olive oil in a large, heavy-based saucepan set over medium heat. Add the onion, garlic, red pepper and carrots along with a pinch of salt. Cook for 10 minutes, until softened. Stir in the chilli powder, cumin and bay leaves and cook for 1 minute, until aromatic.

Increase the heat to high. Add the stock, tomatoes and beans and bring to the boil. Reduce the heat to a medium simmer and cook, uncovered, for about 45 minutes, until the beans are tender.

Serve topped with shredded lettuce, a dollop of sour cream and a few coriander/cilantro leaves. Offer lime wedges on the side for squeezing.

To make this broth more substantial, you could add a scoop of risotto rice at the same time as the broad beans and a little more stock to compensate. If you are using large beans you might want to slip them out of their pale green jackets, but this is a real labour of love!

zesty summer broth

To make the lemon and thyme oil, peel off the lemon zest using a peeler, leaving behind the bitter white pith. Put the zest, thyme and olive oil in a saucepan and heat gently for 10 minutes. Remove from the heat and let cool. Season to taste.

Heat the olive oil in a large saucepan. Peel the zest from the lemon in one large piece so it's easy to find later and add that to the pan. Add the onion, parsley and courgettes/zucchini, cover and cook over low heat, stirring occasionally, for 8 minutes or until softening.

Remove the lemon zest. Add the broad/fava beans and stock, season well and return to the heat for a further 20 minutes.

Transfer a quarter of the soup to a blender, liquidize until smooth, then stir back into the soup. Check the seasoning and add lemon juice to taste.

Divide the soup between 4 bowls, drizzle with lemon and thyme oil and serve with extra parsley and a fresh grinding of black pepper.

2 tablespoons extra virgin olive oil

1 unwaxed lemon

1 onion, chopped

3 tablespoons freshly chopped flat leaf parsley, plus extra to serve

500 g/1 lb. courgettes/zucchini, sliced

300 g/10½ oz. broad/fava beans (podded weight)

800 ml/3⅓ cups vegetable stock

sea salt and freshly ground black pepper

lemon and thyme oil

2 unwaxed lemons

2 fresh thyme or lemon thyme sprigs

250 ml/1 cup extra virgin olive oil

serves 4

This soup has a definite Asian feel to it, with the addition of tamari and sesame oil. But feel free to hold back on the sesame oil and add a sprinkling of grated Parmesan-style cheese on top. The umami (savoury flavour element of the cheese) complements the tamari.

barley & autumn vegetable soup

2 tablespoons butter

1 leek, trimmed and sliced

1 carrot, chopped

250 g/9 oz. peeled pumpkin, chopped

250 g/9 oz. brown mushrooms, sliced

2 medium potatoes, chopped

2 litres/8 cups vegetable stock

200 g/7 oz. pearl or pot barley

¼ teaspoon ground white pepper

2 tablespoons tamari or dark soy sauce

500 g/1 lb. kale, finely shredded

2 spring onions/scallions, thinly sliced on the angle (optional)

1 teaspoon sesame oil

serves 4

Heat the butter in a large saucepan set over medium heat. Add the leek and carrot and cook for 10 minutes, stirring often, until the vegetables have softened. Add the pumpkin, mushrooms, potatoes, stock, barley and pepper and bring to the boil. Reduce the heat to a medium simmer and cook for 45–50 minutes, until the barley is tender. (Pot barley will require a longer cooking time.)

Stir in the tamari and kale and cook for 10 minutes, until the kale is wilted. Serve immediately with a sprinkling of spring onions/scallions (if using) and drizzled with sesame oil .

This is a substantial soup – really more of a light stew. Boiled rice soups are popular in many Asian countries, especially China where they are called congees. They are often eaten for breakfast, but are an acquired taste as the rice is boiled until it breaks down to form a rather viscous white 'porridge'. Spring greens can be the fresh, young outer leaves of brassicas such as cabbage. They work very nicely with the simple Asian flavours here.

garlic & chilli rice soup with spring greens

Put the oils in a saucepan and set over high heat. Add the garlic and spring onions/scallions and cook until the garlic is turning golden and just starting to burn. This will give the soup a lovely, nutty garlic flavour. Add the ginger, chilli and rice to the pan and stir-fry in the garlic-infused oil for 1 minute. Add the stock and soy sauce and bring to the boil.

Cover with a lid and cook over low heat for 30 minutes, until the rice is soft and the soup has thickened. Add the spring greens and cook for 5 minutes, until they turn emerald green and are tender. Ladle the soup into warmed serving bowls, sprinkle the coriander/cilantro over the top and season to taste with pepper.

1 tablespoon vegetable oil

2 teaspoons sesame oil

2 garlic cloves, chopped

4 spring onions/scallions, finely chopped

2 teaspoons finely grated fresh ginger

1 small red chilli, deseeded and thinly sliced

100 g/3½ oz. long-grain white rice

1.5 litres/6 cups vegetable stock

1 tablespoon soy sauce

1 bunch of spring greens, roughly shredded

1 small bunch of fresh coriander/cilantro, chopped

white pepper

serves 2

This is a real winter warmer, perfect for a weekend supper at the end of a cold day. Don't overlook the parsnip – it's a really tasty root veggie and inexpensive too at the right time of year, just when you want to eat it most.

creamy curried parsnip & butter bean soup

2 tablespoons butter

1 onion, chopped

2 garlic cloves, chopped

2 tablespoons mild curry powder

500 g/1 lb. parsnips, chopped

1 litre/4 cups vegetable stock

400-g/14-oz. can butter/lima beans, well drained and rinsed

125 ml/½ cup single cream

1–2 tablespoons freshly snipped chives

sea salt and freshly ground black pepper

warmed flat breads, to serve

serves 4

Heat the butter in a large saucepan set over medium heat. When the butter is sizzling, add the onion and garlic with a pinch of salt and cook for 10 minutes, until the onion has softened.

Stir in the curry powder and cook for 1 minute until aromatic. Add the parsnips, stock and butter/lima beans and bring to the boil. Reduce the heat and simmer, uncovered, for 30 minutes, until the parsnips and beans are tender.

Remove from the heat and let cool for about 10 minutes. Transfer the mixture in batches to a food processor and process until smooth. Return the soup to a clean saucepan and set over low heat. Stir in the cream and season to taste with salt and pepper. Sprinkle over the chives. Serve with warmed flat breads.

As well as making a fantastic soup, the soft and sweet onion mixture here could be added to an egg custard and baked in a pastry case with some soft goats' cheese to make a savoury tart, or spread on a pizza base and topped with black olives and fresh thyme for a classic French pissaladière.

slow-cooked onion & cider soup with cheese toasts

Put the butter in a saucepan set over medium heat. Add the onions and garlic, partially cover with a lid and cook for 20 minutes, stirring often so that the onions become silky soft without burning. Add the stock and cider and bring to the boil. Reduce the heat to low and cook for 40 minutes, until the soup is thick and golden. Remove from the heat and slowly whisk in the egg yolks. Cover and keep warm.

Preheat the grill/broiler to high. Toast the bread under the hot grill/broiler until lightly golden on one side only. Put the cheese slices on the untoasted side and cook under the grill/broiler until the cheese is golden brown and bubbling. Ladle the soup into warmed serving bowls and sit a cheese toast on top of each to serve.

3 tablespoons butter

1 kg/2¼ lbs. onions, sliced

4 garlic cloves

1 litre/4 cups vegetable stock

375 ml/1½ cups sweet cider

2 egg yolks

4 thin slices of baguette or similar

100 g/3½ oz. vegetarian Gruyère cheese (see note on page 4), thinly sliced

serves 4

Despite taking no time at all to prepare, there is something about watercress that seems quintessentially English and refined. Its mustardy bite sits nicely with the intensely flavoured blue cheese. This makes a perfect summery lunch in a flash.

peppery watercress & pea soup with blue cheese

1 small bunch of watercress, about 300 g/10½ oz.

3 tablespoons butter

1 onion, chopped

1 celery stick, chopped

100 g/3½ oz. rocket/arugula

½ teaspoon cracked black pepper

300 g/2 cups peas (frozen or freshly shelled)

1.5 litres/6 cups vegetable stock

100 g/3½ oz. vegetarian blue cheese (see note on page 4)

serves 4

Pick over the watercress to remove any discoloured leaves. Cut off and discard about 5 cm/2 inches from the bottom of the stems. Roughly chop the leaves and remaining stems and set aside.

Put the butter in a large saucepan set over high heat and melt until sizzling. Add the onion and celery and cook for 2–3 minutes, stirring often, until softened. Add the watercress, rocket/arugula and pepper and stir-fry for a couple of minutes until the greens wilt and start to pop in the hot pan. Add the peas and stock and bring to the boil. Reduce the heat and cook at a rapid simmer for 10 minutes, until all the vegetables are very soft. Transfer the mixture to a food processor or blender and whizz until smooth. Pass the mixture through a sieve/strainer into a clean saucepan and gently reheat.

Cut the cheese into 4 pieces and put 1 in the bottom of each of 4 warmed serving bowls. Ladle the hot soup over the top and serve immediately.

A gorgeously coloured and deep-flavoured soup to make in the autumn when squashes, peppers and tomatoes are at their very best and most seasonal. The cumin, rosemary and paprika add a smoky flavour that seems to fit the mood of the season. This is delicious served with some chilli cornbread or simple grilled flat bread.

roasted squash & tomato soup with cumin & rosemary

Preheat the oven to 200°C (400°F) Gas 6. Grease a large baking sheet with 1 tablespoon of the oil. Put the onion slices at one end and scatter over the crushed cumin. Arrange the tomatoes, cut-side-uppermost, over the onions. Put the squash and peppers at the other end of the baking sheet with the garlic. Drizzle the vinegar over the tomatoes, season everything with a little salt and some black pepper and finally drizzle the remaining oil over everything. Roast, uncovered, in the preheated oven for 50–60 minutes, stirring the squash once. Remove from the oven and set aside to cool.

Pop the garlic cloves out of their skins into a large saucepan. Scrape all the roasted vegetables into the saucepan with the oil and add the rosemary and paprika. Stir over low heat for 2–3 minutes and then add the stock and bring to the boil. Reduce the heat and simmer gently for 5–6 minutes. Let cool a little then process or liquidize until smooth. Adjust the seasoning with more cumin, salt and/or lime juice to taste.

Serve piping hot, drizzled with a little extra oil, a sprinkling of crushed roasted cumin and a bread of your choice.

5 tablespoons extra virgin olive oil, plus extra to drizzle

1 large sweet yellow onion, thickly sliced

1 teaspoon crushed cumin seeds, plus extra ground cumin to taste

450 g/1 lb. ripe tomatoes, skinned and halved

450 g/1 lb. prepared squash, cut into 2.5-cm/1-inch chunks

2 medium red bell peppers, halved and deseeded

a small head of garlic, cloves separated but left unpeeled

2–3 teaspoons balsamic vinegar

leaves from 2 small rosemary sprigs, removed from the stalk and very finely chopped

½ teaspoon paprika

1.2 litres/5 cups vegetable stock

freshly squeezed lime juice, to taste (optional)

sea salt and freshly ground black pepper

a pinch of crushed, roasted cumin seeds, to serve

cornbread or flat bread, to serve

serves 4

This salad is all about texture and taste with the added bonus of being simple to prepare and looking stunning. Micro greens look great and have a delicate sweet flavour, but alfalfa or broccoli sprouts are also good.

iceberg, blue cheese & date salad with saffron & walnut dressing

1 iceberg lettuce

200 g/7 oz. vegetarian creamy blue cheese (see note on page 4)

8 dried medjool dates

70 g/½ cup walnuts

a large handful of micro greens (sprouts)

saffron and walnut dressing

½ teaspoon saffron threads

2 tablespoons freshly squeezed orange juice

1 tablespoon white wine vinegar

½ teaspoon sea salt

6 tablespoons walnut oil

serves 6

To make the saffron and walnut dressing, put the saffron and orange juice in a bowl and let infuse for about 10 minutes. Whisk in the vinegar and salt, then the oil, whisking continuously. Cover and set aside until needed.

Slice the lettuce into 8 wedges, then cut each wedge into 3 pieces, giving you a total of 24 pieces. Arrange them in a serving bowl.

Cut the cheese into 12 pieces and arrange these among the lettuce. Chop the dates into 4 and discard the stones. Scatter them over the lettuce along with the walnuts. Pour over the dressing, then scatter over the micro greens. Serve immediately.

This satisfying salad is based on the flavours of Morocco, where chickpeas, beans and lentils are consumed daily. They are cooked in stews, added to couscous, and find their way into salads. This dish is particularly good served warm and is often topped with crumbled goats' cheese from the village.

chickpea salad with onions & paprika

Drain the chickpeas and put them in a deep pan. Cover with water and bring to the boil. Reduce the heat and simmer for about 45 minutes, until the chickpeas are tender but not mushy. Drain the chickpeas and remove any loose skins – you can rub them in a clean tea towel to remove them, or between your fingers.

Tip the warm chickpeas into a bowl. Add the onion, garlic, cumin and paprika and toss in the olive oil and lemon juice while the chickpeas are still warm, making sure they are all well coated. Season with salt and pepper to taste and toss in most of the herbs. Crumble over the goats' cheese, if using, and sprinkle with the rest of the herbs. Serve while still warm with bread.

225 g/8 oz. dried chickpeas, soaked in plenty of cold water overnight

1 red onion, cut in half lengthways, then in half crossways, and sliced with the grain

4 garlic cloves, finely chopped

1 teaspoon ground cumin

1–2 teaspoons paprika

3 tablespoons olive oil

freshly squeezed juice of 1 lemon

a small bunch of fresh flat leaf parsley, coarsely chopped

a small bunch of fresh coriander/cilantro, coarsely chopped

125 g/4½ oz. vegetarian goats' or feta cheese (see note on page 4), crumbled (optional)

sea salt and freshly ground black pepper

bread, to serve

serves 4

This salad, also known as panzanella, is one of the most refreshing for a hot summer's day. It is as light as air and not at all stodgy. The bread soaks up the juices from the vegetables and the olive oil and is sharpened by the touch of vinegar. Mix the basil in at the last moment to prevent it from turning black.

tuscan bread & summer vegetable salad

2 thick slices of stale white country bread, at least 1 day old

4 large very ripe tomatoes, deseeded and diced

1 small red onion, finely chopped

½ cucumber, diced

1 small celery stick, diced

1 garlic clove, crushed

2 tablespoons red wine vinegar

6 tablespoons extra virgin olive oil

20 g/1 oz. fresh basil leaves, roughly torn, plus extra to serve

sea salt and freshly ground black pepper

serves 4

Cut off the crusts from the bread and discard them. Tear the bread into small pieces and put in a bowl. Sprinkle with 1–2 tablespoons cold water – the bread should be only just moist, not soggy. Work the bread with your fingers – like rubbing in butter when making pastry – to distribute the moisture evenly through the bread and break it into smaller crumbs.

Add the tomatoes, onion, cucumber, celery and garlic to the bread and mix lightly. Drizzle with the vinegar, half the olive oil and season well with salt and pepper. Toss very gently. Cover and let stand for 30 minutes so the bread absorbs the flavours.

Lightly mix in the torn basil, then serve drizzled with the remaining olive oil and scattered with extra basil leaves.

This light, fresh country salad is crunchy and tangy, and packed with fresh herbs. It has quite a kick, but you can adjust the chilli quantity if you would prefer it milder. It makes a perfect light lunch served with some crusty bread, fresh from the oven.

country salad with peppers & chillies

In a bowl, mix together the chopped onions, peppers, chillies, celery, garlic, mint and parsley. Add the olive oil and lemon juice and season to taste with salt and pepper. Toss the salad thoroughly and serve immediately.

2 red onions, finely chopped

1 red bell pepper, deseeded and chopped

1 green bell pepper, deseeded and chopped

2 green chillies, deseeded and chopped

2 celery sticks, chopped

2 garlic cloves, chopped

leaves from a large bunch each of fresh mint and flat leaf parsley, chopped

2 tablespoons olive oil

freshly squeezed juice of ½ lemon

sea salt and freshly ground black pepper

crusty bread, to serve

serves 4

This is a slight twist on a classic Greek salad. Butter/lima beans are a staple of Greek cuisine and their delicate flavour works well here with tangy feta and olives. Let sit at room temperature for half an hour before serving.

greek salad with butter beans

400 g/14 oz. cherry tomatoes, halved

50 g/2 oz. kalamata olives, halved and pitted

leaves from a small bunch of fresh mint, roughly chopped

leaves from a small bunch of fresh flat leaf parsley, finely chopped

2 x 410-g cans butter/lima beans, drained and well rinsed

3 tablespoons olive oil

2 red onions, thinly sliced

2 garlic cloves, finely chopped

3 tablespoons freshly squeezed lemon juice

200 g/7 oz. vegetarian feta cheese (see note on page 4), cut into cubes

sea salt and freshly ground black pepper

bread, to serve

serves 4

Put the tomatoes, olives, mint, parsley and beans in a large bowl and toss to combine.

Put the oil in a frying pan set over medium heat. Add the onions and garlic. When they start to sizzle in the oil, remove from the heat and pour over the tomato mixture. Stir in the lemon juice and add the feta. Season to taste with salt and pepper and toss well to combine. Serve at room temperature with bread.

The Indian variety of a comforting potato salad is spicy, crunchy and wonderfully interesting – a perfect quick meal. Add extra lime juice or a different combination or quantity of spice to suit your taste.

indian potato salad

Put 2 tablespoons of the peanut oil in a pan, add the mustard and cumin seeds, cinnamon, chilli and cardamom. Stir-fry until aromatic, then stir in the turmeric. Add the potatoes, salt and pepper and stir-fry for about 2 minutes. Add 250 ml/1 cup water and boil until the liquid has evaporated and the potatoes are tender – add more water if necessary. Sprinkle half the chopped onions over the top and add the coriander/cilantro.

Put the remaining oil in a frying pan, add the onion and the garlic and fry until golden brown. Pour the contents of the pan, and the oil, over the potatoes and toss to coat. Top with the torn coriander/cilantro and serve. Squeeze lime juice over the salad to your own taste.

4 tablespoons peanut oil or ghee

1 tablespoon mustard seeds

½ tablespoon cumin seeds

½ cinnamon stick, crushed

1 dried red chilli, crushed

6 cardamom pods, crushed

1 teaspoon turmeric

500 g/1 lb. potatoes, cut into chunks

2 red onions, chopped

1 garlic clove, crushed

a handful of fresh coriander/ cilantro, torn

salt and freshly ground black pepper

lime wedges, to serve

serves 4

You need to be careful when buying ricotta because it can sometimes be very soggy, especially when sold in tubs. Mozzarella also works well, as does a soft, fresh goats' cheese. Leave some seeds in the chilli to give a little kick, awaken the other flavours and contrast with the sweet nuts.

1 star anise

1 cinnamon stick

2 pears, unpeeled, quartered and cored

150 g/5½ oz. prepared salad leaves, such as rocket/arugula, shredded radicchio or baby Swiss chard

125 g/4½ oz. vegetarian ricotta cheese (see note on page 4)

honeyed pecans

50 g/2 oz. pecans

¼ teaspoon dried chilli/hot pepper flakes

¼ teaspoon fennel seeds

3 tablespoons clear honey

dressing

4 tablespoons sunflower/safflower oil

1 tablespoon walnut oil

freshly squeezed juice of 1 lemon

1 large red chilli, partly deseeded and chopped

serves 4

winter-spiced salad with pears, honeyed pecans & ricotta

Fill a saucepan with water and add the star anise and cinnamon. Bring to the boil and add the pears. Poach for 12 minutes, or until tender.

Put the pecans, a large pinch of salt, the chilli/hot pepper flakes and the fennel seeds in a frying pan and toast until golden and aromatic. Pour in the honey, turn the heat right up and leave to bubble away for a few minutes. Tip onto greaseproof paper and let cool.

To make the dressing, whisk together the sunflower/safflower and walnut oils, the lemon juice and chilli.

Transfer the salad leaves to bowls, scatter over the pears and crumble over the ricotta. Drizzle with the dressing. Roughly break up the nuts with your fingers and scatter them over the top.

omelettes & frittatas

A strong blue cheese adds a powerful flavour to this omelette. However if you prefer a more delicate flavour, try using smooth, creamy-textured vegetarian dolcelatte. Dolcelatte is quite soft and will not crumble, so is best chopped into small pieces before adding.

caramelized onion & blue cheese omelette

Put half the butter and oil in the omelette pan and heat until the butter has melted. Add the onion and fry gently for about 10 minutes, until golden and caramelized, stirring occasionally.

Meanwhile, break the eggs into a bowl and whisk briefly with a fork, just enough to mix the yolks and whites. Season with salt and pepper. Using a slotted spoon, add the onions to the eggs and mix gently.

Increase the heat to medium-high and add the remaining butter and oil if necessary. When the pan is hot, pour in the omelette mixture. Using a spatula or back of a fork, draw the mixture from the sides to the centre as it sets. Let the liquid flow and fill the space at the sides.

Sprinkle the cheese over the top, fold over a third of the omelette to the centre, then fold over the remaining third. Slide onto a warmed plate and serve immediately.

1 tablespoon unsalted butter

1 tablespoon sunflower oil

1 small onion, halved and thinly sliced

3 large eggs

40 g/1½ oz. vegetarian blue cheese (see note on page 4), crumbled

sea salt and freshly ground black pepper

an 18-cm/7-inch heavy omelette pan

serves 1

The secret of a good tortilla is to soften the potatoes in lots of olive oil and then add them to the eggs and back into the pan, not the other way around. If you pour the eggs directly over the potatoes in the pan, they will not coat the potatoes evenly and you will get air bubbles. Don't rush the cooking either – the egg proteins will get agitated, resulting in a tough texture rather than a creamy finish.

tortilla with potatoes, chillies & roasted pimentos

6 tablespoons olive oil

600 g/1½ lb. (about 4) potatoes, peeled and thinly sliced

2 red chillies, thinly sliced

1 onion, thinly sliced

½ teaspoon sea salt

8 eggs

125 g/4½ oz. marinated roasted pimentos, drained and sliced

a 20-cm/8-inch non-stick ovenproof frying pan, at least 7 cm/3 inches deep

serves 6

Heat 4 tablespoons of the oil in the frying pan, then add the potatoes, chillies, onion and salt. Reduce the heat to low and cover with a lid. Cook for 15 minutes, stirring occasionally so the onions don't catch on the base of the pan.

Preheat the grill/broiler.

Beat the eggs in a large mixing bowl. Transfer the cooked ingredients from the frying pan to the beaten eggs and stir. Add the roasted pimentos, and stir again.

Turn the heat up to medium under the frying pan and add the remaining oil. Pour the egg mixture into the pan. Cook for 4–5 minutes until the base is golden – loosen the sides and lift up to check.

Grill/broil for 3–4 minutes, until it is cooked all the way through. Cut into wedges and serve.

Mushrooms are great for a filling meal, especially when combined with potatoes as in this satisfying tortilla. Field mushrooms are given as a guide, but you can substitute for whatever varieties you prefer or are available.

field mushroom tortilla

Heat the butter and olive oil in an ovenproof frying pan, add the potatoes and brown on all sides. Transfer to a plate, then cook the mushrooms on both sides for 5 minutes, adding a little more oil or butter if necesary. Transfer to another plate and return the potatoes to the pan. Sprinkle in the garlic, then add the mushrooms and spinach.

Mix the eggs and milk together, season and pour into the pan. Cover and cook gently for 5 minutes.

Preheat the grill/broiler to medium-high.

Grill/broil the tortilla for 6–8 minutes, or until golden on top. Check that the egg is set, then serve hot or cold.

20 g/1 oz. butter

2 tablespoons olive oil

3 cooked potatoes, diced

200 g/7 oz. flat field mushrooms

1 garlic clove, crushed

125 g/4½ oz. young spinach

4 eggs

100 ml/½ cup milk

sea salt and freshly ground black pepper

serves 4–6

Although potato is the traditional ingredient in a Spanish omelette, chickpeas are a delicious alternative, adding a slightly sweet, nutty flavour. This tortilla is quite filling, so is ideal as a main meal; serve it with a crisp green salad and a glass of red wine.

chickpea tortilla

5 large eggs

½ teaspoon sweet Spanish paprika (pimenton dulce)

3 tablespoons chopped fresh flat leaf parsley

3 tablespoons extra virgin olive oil

1 large onion, finely chopped

1 red bell pepper, halved, deseeded and chopped

2 garlic cloves, finely chopped

400-g/14-oz. can chickpeas, rinsed and well drained

sea salt and freshly ground black pepper

a 20-cm/8-inch heavy non-stick frying pan

serves 2–3

Break the eggs into a large bowl, add salt, pepper and paprika and whisk briefly with a fork. Stir in the chopped parsley.

Heat 2 tablespoons of the oil in the frying pan. Add the onion and red pepper and cook for about 5 minutes until softened, turning frequently. Add the garlic and chickpeas and cook for 2 minutes.

Transfer to the bowl of eggs and stir gently. Add the remaining oil to the pan and return to the heat. Add the chickpea mixture, spreading it evenly in the pan. Cook over medium-low heat until the bottom is golden brown and the top almost set.

Put a plate or flat saucepan lid on top of the pan and hold it in place. Invert the pan so the tortilla drops onto the plate or lid. Slide back into the pan, brown side up, and cook for another 2–3 minutes until lightly browned on the other side. Cut into wedges and serve.

This frittata has a real Mediterranean feel and is flavoured with some of Italy's favourite ingredients – olives, sun-dried tomatoes and a hard Parmesan-style cheese. If you have the time, it is worth mixing the tomatoes and sage into the eggs up to an hour before cooking for a more intense flavour.

sun-dried tomato frittata

Break the eggs into a large bowl and whisk briefly with a fork. Add the sun-dried tomatoes, sage, olives, Parmesan, salt and pepper and mix.

Heat the oil in the frying pan, add the onion and cook over low heat until soft and golden.

Increase the heat to moderate, pour the egg mixture into the pan and stir just long enough to mix in the onion. Cook over medium-low heat until the base of the frittata is golden and the top has almost set.

Preheat the grill/broiler.

Slide the pan under the hot grill/broiler to finish cooking or put a plate or flat saucepan lid on top of the pan and invert the pan so the frittata drops onto the plate or lid. Return the frittata to the pan, cooked side up, and cook on top of the stove for 1–2 minutes.

Transfer to a serving plate, top with cheese shavings, if using, and serve hot or cold, cut into wedges.

6 large eggs

8 sun-dried tomatoes in oil, drained and sliced

1 tablespoon chopped fresh sage leaves

50 g/2 oz. pitted black olives, thickly sliced

50 g/2 oz. freshly grated Parmesan-style cheese (see note on page 4), plus extra shavings to serve (optional)

2 tablespoons extra virgin olive oil

1 onion, halved and sliced

sea salt and freshly ground black pepper

a 20-cm/8-inch non-stick ovenproof frying pan

serves 2–3

Ideal for a lunch or supper dish, or perfect for al fresco dining served with a crisp salad, this omelette is just bursting with flavour. It is worth buying tomatoes ripened on the vine for their extra taste explosion.

feta cheese & tomato open omelette

5 large eggs

2 tablespoons chopped fresh basil

1 tablespoon chopped fresh mint

3 spring onions/scallions, finely chopped

2 tablespoons sunflower oil

75 g/2½ oz vegetarian feta cheese (see note on page 4), crumbled

8 small cherry tomatoes, halved

sea salt and freshly ground black pepper

an 18-cm/7-inch heavy ovenproof omelette pan

serves 2

Break the eggs into a bowl and whisk briefly with a fork, just enough to mix the yolks and whites. Season with salt and pepper, add 2 tablespoons water, the basil, mint and spring onions/scallions and mix briefly.

Heat the oil in the omelette pan. Pour in the egg mixture and cook over medium heat for 4–5 minutes, drawing the mixture from the sides to the centre until the omelette is half cooked.

Top with the feta and the tomato halves, cut side up, and cook for 2 minutes.

Preheat the grill/broiler.

Slide under the hot grill/broiler and cook until light golden brown. Slide onto a warmed plate and serve immediately.

It's so easy to cook too much spaghetti, so this frittata is a great way to use up any leftovers. Mixed with a fresh arrabbiata sauce made with tomatoes and fiery chillies it has a real kick.

spicy spaghetti frittata

Heat 1 tablespoon of the oil in a saucepan, add the onion and sauté for 5 minutes until softened. Add the garlic, tomatoes and chilli and cook for 3–4 minutes, stirring several times. Add the tomato purée/paste and wine or water and simmer for 5 minutes. Remove from the heat, add the spaghetti and toss gently.

Break the eggs into a large bowl and whisk briefly with a fork. Add the spaghetti and sauce and mix gently.

Heat the remaining oil in the frying pan, add the spaghetti and egg mixture and cook over low heat for 10–12 minutes, or until golden brown on the underside and almost set on the top.

Preheat the grill/broiler.

Sprinkle the frittata with the cheese and slide under the hot grill/broiler for 30–60 seconds to melt the cheese and finish cooking the top. Let cool for 5 minutes, then transfer to a plate. Put the rocket/arugula leaves on top of the frittata, sprinkle with balsamic vinegar and serve.

3 tablespoons extra virgin olive oil

1 onion, chopped

1 garlic clove, crushed

3 ripe plum tomatoes, chopped

1 fresh red chilli, deseeded and finely chopped

2 tablespoons tomato purée/paste

150 ml/⅔ cup white wine or water

325 g/2–2½ cups cold cooked spaghetti (140 g/5 oz. before cooking)

6 large eggs

2 tablespoons freshly grated Parmesan-style hard cheese (see note on page 4)

a small handful of rocket/arugula leaves

2 tablespoons balsamic vinegar

sea salt and freshly ground black pepper

a 24-cm/12-inch heavy non-stick ovenproof frying pan

serves 4

The frittata is Italy's version of a flat, open-faced omelette. This one is simply flavoured with fresh mint and courgettes/zucchini. The courgettes/zucchini can be coarsely grated rather than sliced, but make sure you squeeze out any excess water before adding to the pan.

minted courgette frittata

6 large eggs

2 tablespoons chopped fresh mint

250 g/8 oz. baby new potatoes, thickly sliced

2 tablespoons extra virgin olive or sunflower/safflower oil

1 large onion, chopped

4 courgettes/zucchini, sliced

sea salt and freshly ground black pepper

a 24-cm/12-inch heavy ovenproof frying pan

serves 3–4

Break the eggs into a bowl and whisk briefly with a fork. Season well with salt and pepper. Mix in the chopped mint.

Cook the potatoes in a saucepan of boiling, salted water until just tender. Drain thoroughly.

Meanwhile, heat the oil in the frying pan, add the onion and cook gently for about 10 minutes, until soft and pale golden. Add the courgettes/zucchini and stir over low heat for 3–4 minutes until just softened. Add the potatoes and mix gently.

Pour the eggs over the vegetables and cook over low heat until the frittata is lightly browned underneath and has almost set on top.

Preheat the grill/broiler.

Slide the frittata under the hot grill/broiler for 30–60 seconds, to set the top. Serve, cut into wedges.

Perfectly set eggs spiked with the fragrance of mixed fresh herbs make a perfect quick supper dish. Dot the frittata with a little ricotta just before the top is grilled/broiled. Cut into small squares, frittata makes great finger food.

frittata with fresh herbs & ricotta

Put the eggs into a bowl, add the herbs, celery salt, if using, and a good sprinkling of salt and pepper. Beat with a fork.

Preheat the grill/broiler.

Heat the oil in a non-stick ovenproof frying pan until hot, then add the egg mixture. Fry over medium heat for 5–6 minutes until almost set. Dot the ricotta over the top and cook under the hot grill/broiler until the surface is set and browned.

Let cool slightly, then cut into wedges and serve warm.

6 eggs

a large handful of chopped mixed fresh herbs, such as basil, chervil, chives, marjoram, mint and/or parsley

1 teaspoon celery salt (optional)

2 tablespoons extra virgin olive oil

125 g/4½ oz. vegetarian ricotta cheese (see note on page 4), crumbled into big pieces

sea salt and freshly ground black pepper

serves 4

Ideally, frittatas should be cooked slowly, only lightly coloured and still slightly moist when served. This recipe flashes the frittata under the grill/broiler to set the top. Use little waxy potatoes, which are creamy and yellow and sweeter than most larger varieties, partnered with tenderstem broccoli.

tenderstem broccoli & potato frittata

8 small waxy potatoes, (such as Kipfler), quartered

250 ml/1 cup vegetable stock

60 ml/¼ cup light olive oil

250 g/8 oz. tenderstem or baby broccoli, trimmed and halved lengthways

1 red onion, thinly sliced

8 eggs

100 g/1 cup grated Parmesan-style cheese (see note on page 4)

mixed leaf salad, to serve

serves 4

Put the potatoes in a large non-stick ovenproof frying pan and pour over the stock. Put the pan over high heat and bring the stock to the boil. Boil for 10 minutes, turning the potatoes often, until almost all the stock has been absorbed.

Add the olive oil, broccoli and onion to the pan and cook for 1 minute, turning the vegetables to coat in the oil. Cover and cook for just 2–3 minutes, to soften the broccoli.

Preheat the grill/broiler to high.

Beat the eggs with half of the cheese and pour over the vegetables. Cover the pan and cook over medium heat for 8–10 minutes, until the eggs look set.

Sprinkle over the remaining cheese, then place under the hot grill/boiler and cook until the top of the frittata is golden. Let cool slightly before removing from the pan.

Cut into wedges and serve with a mixed leaf salad.

Variation Top the frittata with 100 g/3½ oz. strong-flavoured vegetarian cheese, such as fontina, just before putting it under the hot grill/broiler, so that it melts and gives the frittata a gooey and golden topping.

pasta

This pasta is packed with delcious, nutritious vegetables. Roasting the aubergine/eggplant, tomatoes and garlic in the oven before adding them to the pasta sauce means they have the chance to caramelize and become really sweet.

roasted vegetable pasta

Preheat the oven to 200°C (400°F) Gas 6.

Put the aubergine/eggplant, tomatoes and garlic into a large roasting pan. Add 2 tablespoons of the olive oil and mix. Sprinkle with salt and pepper and cook in the preheated oven for 30–40 minutes, turning the vegetables from time to time, until the aubergine/eggplant is tender and golden.

Meanwhile, bring a large saucepan of water to the boil. Add a good pinch of salt, then the pasta, and cook until al dente, or according to the timings on the packet.

Drain the pasta well and return it to the warm pan. Add the roasted aubergine/eggplant and tomatoes, then the shallot, coriander/cilantro, mint and lime juice. Add the remaining oil and toss well to mix. Divide between 4 bowls or plates and serve.

2 aubergines/eggplants, cut into 2.5-cm/1-inch cubes

500 g/1 lb. ripe tomatoes, quartered

2 garlic cloves, halved

4 tablespoons olive oil

300 g/10¼ oz. dried pasta, such as fusilli or fusilli bucati

1 shallot, finely chopped

2 tablespoons chopped fresh coriander/cilantro

2 tablespoons chopped fresh mint

freshly squeezed juice of 1 lime

salt and freshly ground black pepper

serves 4

This hearty soup of pasta and beans is a classic from the Puglia region of Italy and makes a substantial meal. In this version the beans are replaced with creamy chickpeas. The pasta shapes traditionally used are orecchiette, meaning 'little ears' but any small shape will work just as well.

pasta e fagioli

250 g/9 oz. dried chickpeas

2 tablespoons olive oil

1 onion, finely chopped

2 garlic cloves, finely chopped

a sprig of fresh rosemary

¼ teaspoon dried chilli/hot pepper flakes

400-g/14-oz can chopped tomatoes

1 tablespoon tomato purée/paste

1.5 litres/6 cups vegetable stock

100 g/3½ oz. small pasta shapes such as orecchiette or conchigliette

sea salt and freshly ground black pepper

freshly grated Parmesan-style cheese (see note on page 4), to serve

extra virgin olive oil, to serve

serves 4

Soak the chickpeas in cold water overnight. Drain and put in a large saucepan with sufficient cold water to cover. Bring to the boil, reduce the heat to medium and cook, uncovered, for 45 minutes, until very tender. Drain and set aside.

Heat the oil in a large, heavy-based saucepan set over medium heat. Add the onion, garlic, rosemary and chilli/hot pepper flakes along with a pinch of salt and cook for 8–10 minutes, stirring often, until the onion has softened.

Increase the heat to high. Stir in the tomatoes, tomato purée/paste, stock and the chickpeas and bring to the boil. Add the pasta, reduce the heat to a medium simmer and cook for about 20 minutes, until the pasta is tender. Season to taste with salt and pepper.

Serve sprinkled with cheese and drizzled with olive oil.

This pasta-based salad is packed with Mediterranean flavours and is perfect way to appreciate sweet summer peppers. This recipe lends itself to a large occasion because the vegetables and bread can be prepared in advance, then left overnight to soak up the flavours of the olive oil, garlic and vinegar. As the guests are due, toss in the pasta, basil, salt and pepper. If you don't have ciabatta, stale bread also works well.

trottole pasta salad with peppers & garlic

Put the tomato, peppers, bread and garlic in a large bowl with the olive oil and vinegar. Leave for a couple of hours or overnight to develop the flavours.

Cook the pasta according to the timings on the packet. Cool with cold water, then mix into the vegetables. Stir in the chopped basil, season to taste and serve.

1 beef tomato, cut into tiny cubes

½ red bell pepper, halved, deseeded, then cut into tiny squares

½ yellow bell pepper, halved, deseeded, then cut into tiny squares

½ orange bell pepper, halved, deseeded, then cut into tiny squares

100 g/3½ oz. ciabatta bread, cut into tiny pieces

2 garlic cloves, crushed

200 ml/¾ cup good-quality extra virgin olive oil

2 tablespoons balsamic vinegar

400 g/14 oz. spiral pasta, such as trottole or fusilli

a large bunch of basil leaves, coarsely chopped

sea salt and freshly ground black pepper

serves 6–8

Young asparagus is one of life's great gifts, but don't miss its rather short seasonal window. Because it is such a treat, keep it simple with this one-pot pasta, combining the prime spears with just a handful of other fresh, good-quality ingredients for a delicious fuss-free meal.

asparagus tagliatelle

250 ml/1 cup single/light cream

300 g/10½ oz. tagliatelle pasta, or simliar

1 bunch of fine asparagus, trimmed and each spear cut into 4 pieces

grated zest and freshly squeezed juice of 1 unwaxed lemon

3 tablespoons finely chopped flat leaf parsley

100 g/3½ oz. finely grated Parmesan-style cheese (see note on page 4)

sea salt and freshly ground black pepper

serves 2

Put the cream in a small saucepan and bring to the boil. Reduce the heat to a low simmer and cook for 8–10 minutes, until slightly thickened. Set aside.

Cook the pasta according to the packet instructions. About 2 minutes before the pasta is cooked, add the asparagus to the boiling water. Drain well and return to the warm pan with the reduced cream, lemon zest and juice, parsley and half of the cheese. Toss together, season well with sea salt and black pepper and serve with the remaining cheese sprinkled on top.

Variation Instead of asparagus, pan-fry 1 grated courgette/zucchini in 1 tablespoon of butter over medium heat until softened and golden. Add the courgette/zucchini to the well-drained pasta along with the other ingredients.

The toasted pecan nuts add texture to this rich and creamy cheese sauce. Blue cheese is perfect combined with the milder mascarpone, but be sure to check that the cheese you use is vegetarian-friendly.

penne with blue cheese, pecan & mascarpone sauce

Cook the pasta according to the instructions on the packet.

While the pasta is cooking, melt the butter in a saucepan and gently fry the garlic over low heat for 2–3 minutes, or until soft but not browned. Stir in the cheeses, mace and a little seasoning. Cook gently until the sauce is heated through but the cheese still has a little texture.

Remove the pan from the heat and stir in the pecan nuts and chives. Stir into the cooked, drained pasta. Season to taste and serve hot.

300 g/10½ oz. penne pasta

2 tablespoons unsalted butter

1 garlic clove, peeled and crushed

175 g/6 oz. vegetarian blue cheese (see note on page 4), crumbled

175 g/6 oz. mascarpone cheese

a pinch of ground mace or a little freshly grated nutmeg

100 g/3½ oz. pecan nuts, toasted and roughly chopped

2 tablespoons snipped fresh chives

sea salt and freshly ground black pepper

serves 4

This dish is perfect for a late brunch, and is super easy to whip up. You could also add a splash of vodka to the shallots too, which just gives it a slight acidic edge, as wine does. Make sure you go for unwaxed lemons so you are not ingesting all the horrid chemicals on waxed ones.

linguine with lemon, basil & cream

2 tablespoons butter

2 shallots, finely chopped

1 unwaxed lemon

300 ml/1¼ cups whipping cream

200 ml/¾ cup hot vegetable stock

2 handfuls of fresh basil leaves, plus more to serve

350 g/12 oz. dried linguine

75 g/2½ oz. Parmesan-style cheese shavings, plus extra to serve (see note on page 4)

sea salt and freshly ground black pepper

serves 4

Heat the butter in a frying pan and add the shallots. Add a pinch of salt, cover and cook over low heat for 6–7 minutes, stirring every now and then, until soft and glossy.

Put a large saucepan of water on to boil for the pasta. Meanwhile, take a potato peeler and pare off the zest of the lemon, leaving behind the white pith. Try to pare the zest in one long piece so you can easily remove it later.

Add the cream, stock, lemon zest and basil to the shallots and gently simmer for 10–15 minutes, uncovered, until it has reduced and thickened – it should only just coat the back of a spoon. Cook the linguine in the boiling water until al dente.

Fish out the lemon zest and season the sauce with a little salt and lots of pepper. Drain the pasta and return to the pan. Stir in the cheese and squeeze in some juice from the lemon. Add more juice or seasoning, to taste. Garnish with more basil and cheese shavings and serve.

Crumbly goats' cheese works surprisingly well in pesto, adding a slightly creamy edge to it. Roughly crumble it in so you get pockets of the molten cheese tucked in amongst your tangle of tagliatelle.

tagliatelle with peas & goats' cheese pesto

To make the pesto, put the garlic, chillies, basil and a large pinch of salt in a food processor and process until roughly chopped. Alternatively, crush everything with a pestle and mortar.

Put the pine nuts in a dry frying pan and toast over low heat for a few minutes, shaking the pan, until they are golden all over. Add the pine nuts to the mixture in the food processor (or the mortar) and process again until coarsely chopped. Add half the olive oil and process again. Add the remaining oil, crumble in the goats' cheese and stir. Taste and season.

Bring a large saucepan of salted water and a small pan of unsalted water to the boil. Add the peas to the smaller pan and simmer for 4–5 minutes if fresh or 3 minutes if frozen. Once the water in the large pot comes to a rolling boil, add the tagliatelle and cook until it is al dente. Drain and tip back into the pan.

Add 2–3 good dollops of pesto and the peas to the tagliatelle and toss through the hot strands, then add the remaining pesto making sure all the pasta is thoroughly coated. Transfer to bowls and sprinkle with basil and freshly grated cheese.

250 g/9 oz. fresh or frozen peas, defrosted

400 g/14 oz. tagliatelle

sea salt and freshly ground black pepper

freshly grated Parmesan-style cheese (see note on page 4), to serve

pesto

1 small garlic clove

2 large green chillies, deseeded

40 g/1½ oz. fresh basil leaves, plus extra to serve

25 g/1 oz. pine nuts

100 ml/½ cup extra virgin olive oil

100 g/3½ oz. goats' cheese

serves 4

The light texture and creamy flavour of ricotta cheese makes the perfect backdrop to walnuts and fresh, crisp broccoli in this deliciously simple pasta. The lemon zest and juice lift the whole dish.

spaghetti with broccoli, walnuts & ricotta

100 g/3½ oz. walnut halves

1 head of broccoli (about 400–500 g/14–16 oz.)

3 tablespoons light olive oil

3 garlic cloves, thinly sliced

1 handful of fresh flat leaf parsley, chopped

finely grated zest and freshly squeezed juice of 1 unwaxed lemon

200 g/7 oz. vegetarian ricotta cheese (see note on page 4)

400 g/14 oz. spaghetti

sea salt and freshly ground black pepper

serves 4

Preheat the oven to 180°C (350°F) Gas 4.

Spread the walnuts out on a baking sheet and roast in the preheated oven for about 8 minutes, shaking the sheet occasionally, until they start to brown.

To prepare the broccoli, trim off the gnarly part, about 2.5 cm/1 inch from the stem end, and discard. Thinly slice the stem until you reach the point where it starts to branch into florets. Finally, slice off the individual florets.

Heat the oil in a frying pan, add the brocolli stems and cook for about 2–3 minutes, turning often, then add the florets and cook for about 5 minutes, until the broccoli has softened. Add the garlic, parsley, lemon zest and walnuts and cook for 5 minutes, stirring often. Reduce the heat to medium and stir through the ricotta and lemon juice. Season well with salt and pepper and leave in the pan to keep warm.

Cook the spaghetti according to the packet instructions. Drain and return it to the warm pan with the sauce. Stir gently to combine and serve immediately.

This tasty pasta is inspired by the classic Italian dish of pumpkin-filled ravioli with sage butter except this is an inside-out version and therefore much easier to make! The recipe uses butternut squash, but you could use any winter squash, including pumpkin.

spaghetti with butternut squash & sage

Put the oil in a frying pan and set over high heat. Add the squash and cook for 5–6 minutes, turning often, until golden but not breaking up. Add the garlic and sage to the pan and cook for 2–3 minutes. Remove from the heat and let sit to allow the flavours to develop.

Cook the pasta according to the packet instructions. Drain well and return to the warm pan with the squash mixture. Add the parsley and half of the pecorino and season well with salt and pepper. Serve immediately with the remaining cheese sprinkled over the top.

65 ml/¼ cup light olive oil

400 g/14 oz. butternut squash, peeled, deseeded and cut into thin wedges

2 garlic cloves, chopped

10–12 small fresh sage leaves

400 g/14 oz. spaghetti

1 handful of fresh flat leaf parsley, chopped

50 g/1¾ oz. Parmesan-style cheese, grated (see note on page 4)

sea salt and freshly ground black pepper

serves 4

This recipe is from Cyprus and uses orzo pasta rather than rice, which is more commonly used in pilafs. Rather than boiling the pasta, it is baked in the oven like a casserole, which makes it a very simple dish to prepare.

orzo pilaf

2 tablespoons extra virgin olive oil

1 onion, chopped

2 garlic cloves, crushed

250 g/9 oz. orzo pasta

400-g/14-oz. can whole peeled tomatoes

300 ml/1¼ cups vegetable stock

a handful of fresh flat leaf parsley, chopped

sea salt and freshly ground black pepper

a lidded casserole dish

serves 4

Preheat the oven to 200°C (400°F) Gas 6.

Put the oil and onion in a lidded casserole dish over medium heat. Stir and cook until soft, 3–5 minutes. Add the garlic and orzo and stir until coated with the oil. Add the tomatoes, stock and parsley and stir well, breaking up the tomatoes with a wooden spoon.

Cover the casserole dish with the lid and bake in the preheated oven until the pasta is tender and most of the liquid has been absorbed, 20–25 minutes. Serve hot.

noodles & stir-fries

This simple but delicious dish is the perfect one-pot option when catering for vegetarian guests, so don't be daunted by this large mountain – they'll love it. Other vegetables can always be added, such as asparagus, baby corn, thin green beans, carrots, mushrooms or water chestnuts.

noodle mountain

Cook the noodles according to the timings on the packet, drain and transfer to a bowl of cold water until needed.

Heat the oil in a wok and add the garlic, ginger, onions and chillies. Cook over medium heat for 5 minutes until softened. Add the cabbage and beansprouts and stir briefly. Drain the noodles well and add to the wok. Toss with 2 large spoons, then add the soy sauce, lime juice, spring onions/scallions and cashew nuts. Mix well and serve.

300 g/10½ oz. dried egg noodles

6 tablespoons vegetable oil

4 garlic cloves, crushed and chopped

12-cm/4½-inch piece fresh ginger, peeled and chopped

4 onions, finely sliced

4 chillies, finely chopped

1 Chinese cabbage, finely shredded

250 g/9 oz. beansprouts

200 ml/¾ cup soy sauce

freshly squeezed juice of 4 limes

2 bunches of spring onions/ scallions, chopped

400 g/14 oz. cashew nuts, chopped

serves 20

Deep-fried tofu cakes are available from Asian stores or health-food stores where they can be found in the refrigerator. You can substitute ordinary firm tofu, cut into cubes instead.

stir-fried tofu with chilli coconut sauce

1 tablespoon sesame oil

1 onion, sliced

200 g/7 oz. green beans, cut into 5-cm/2-inch lengths

350 g/12 oz. deep-fried tofu, sliced

2 tablespoons sweet chilli sauce

1 handful of fresh basil leaves, preferably Thai basil

2 tablespoons sesame seeds, toasted in a dry frying pan

sauce

400 ml/1⅔ cups coconut milk

300 ml/1¼ cups vegetable stock

2 stalks lemongrass, sliced crossways

1 tablespoon soy sauce

8 lime leaves, sliced

2 garlic cloves, chopped

3-cm/1¼-inch piece fresh ginger, peeled and grated

serves 4

Put all the sauce ingredients into a large saucepan, bring to the boil and simmer for 20 minutes until reduced by half. Strain the sauce and reserve.

Heat the oil in a wok or frying pan and stir-fry the onions and beans for 1 minute. Add the tofu cakes and stir-fry for a further 1 minute. Add the coconut sauce, sweet chilli sauce and basil leaves and heat through. Serve sprinkled with the sesame seeds.

Fat and chewy wheat-based Japanese udon noodles make for a wonderfully satisfying meal. Oyster sauce is available in vegetarian versions, where the complexity of flavour comes from shiitake mushrooms. Find it in from Asian stores or specialist online retailers. The sauce flavours are absorbed by the tofu in this delicious aromatic dish.

udon noodles with tofu & shiitake mushrooms

Bring a saucepan of water to the boil. Throw in the noodles and cook according to the timings on the packet. Drain and rinse under cold running water. Set aside.

Combine all the sauce ingredients in a bowl and set aside.

Heat the oil in a wok or large frying pan until hot. Add the tofu to the pan in batches and stir-fry over high heat until golden all over. Remove the tofu from the wok and drain on kitchen paper.

Add the ginger, shredded spring onions/scallions and chilli to the wok and stir-fry for 1 minute, then throw in the shiitake mushrooms. Cook for 1 more minute, then pour in the sauce and bring to the boil. Reduce the heat, return the tofu to the wok and simmer gently for 1–2 minutes, or until the sauce has thickened.

Stir the drained noodles into the wok very carefully, then heat through until piping hot. Remove from the heat and divide equally between 2 bowls. Garnish with the remaining spring onions/scallions and serve.

400 g/14 oz. fresh udon noodles

2 tablespoons vegetable oil

300 g/10½ oz. firm tofu, cut into 2-cm/1-inch cubes

2-cm/1-inch piece of fresh ginger, peeled and shredded

3 spring onions/scallions, white parts cut into 2-cm/1-inch lengths and shredded, and green parts sliced on the diagonal

1 red chilli, deseeded and shredded

200 g/7 oz. shiitake mushrooms, stalks discarded and caps sliced

sauce

2 tablespoons vegetarian 'oyster' sauce

1 tablespoon light soy sauce

150 ml/⅔ cup vegetable stock

1 tablespoon cornflour/cornstarch, combined with 2 tablespoons cold water

serves 2

This dish is incredibly versatile. Mushrooms, mangetout, broccoli, baby corn or Chinese leaf all work well – use whatever is in season, or more to the point, what's in the refrigerator! The same applies to the noodles. Buckwheat noodles are ideal because they thicken the dish slightly and have a gorgeous nutty flavour, but substitute your favourite – the choice is endless with both fresh and dried noodles.

buckwheat noodles in miso ginger broth

175 g/6 oz. buckwheat noodles

1 teaspoon sesame oil

1 tablespoon sunflower/safflower oil

1 red onion, finely chopped

1 red chilli, deseeded and finely chopped

2.5-cm/1-inch piece fresh ginger, peeled and grated

4 tablespoons soy sauce

1 litre/4 cups vegetable stock

150 g/5½ oz. green beans, topped

150 g/5½ oz. carrots, cut into matchsticks

125 g/4½ oz. oyster mushrooms, thickly sliced

225 g/8 oz. bok choy, cut into thick rounds

3 tablespoons miso paste

100 g/3½ oz. enoki mushrooms, root base removed

7 spring onions/scallions, cut lengthways into strips

150 g/5½ oz. beansprouts, rinsed and drained

serves 4

Cook the buckwheat noodles according to the timings on the packet, then rinse well.

Put the sesame and sunflower/safflower oils, onion, chilli, ginger and soy sauce in a large saucepan. Cook gently for 10 minutes until the onion is soft, then stir in the stock and beans. Bring gently to the boil, then add the carrots and oyster mushrooms. Continue cooking for 2–3 minutes, then add the bok choy and cooked noodles. Continue simmering for 1–2 minutes. Add the miso, enoki mushrooms, spring onions/scallions and beansprouts then serve immediately while the vegetables are still crunchy and vibrant in colour.

Notes Miso is a fermented paste of soya beans. There are various types depending on the culture used to ferment the beans – barley, rice and wheat are all available. The miso is stirred in at the end of the cooking process so that its nutritional content is not diminished.

Enoki mushrooms are small mushrooms with long stems and tiny white caps. They are usually bought in clumps with the root base still attached – this is removed before cooking.

If you are using fresh noodles, there is no need to precook them. Simply stir them in with the bok choy.

Szechuan peppercorns are an important spice in Chinese cookery. Not related to black pepper, Szechuan peppercorns are unusual in appearance and taste. They are reddish berries, usually opened out, containing black shiny seeds which should be discarded. The berries smell fruity and woody at the same time with a peculiarly numbing bite, quite unlike regular pepper. They are readily available in Chinese stores. Serve this dish with noodles or rice.

vegetable stir-fry with szechuan peppercorns

Discard any shiny black inner seeds from the peppercorns. Toast the peppercorns in a small frying pan over low heat for 1–2 minutes until aromatic. Using a mortar and pestle, grind to a coarse powder.

Heat the peanut oil in a wok and add the spring onions/scallions and garlic. Stir-fry over medium-high heat for 1 minute. Add the pepper, carrot, baby corn, lemon juice and 1 tablespoon of the soy sauce and stir-fry for 2–3 minutes.

Add the broccoli, sugar snap peas, ground Szechuan pepper and the remaining soy sauce. Stir-fry briefly, cover and cook for 4–5 minutes or until the vegetables are tender but still firm. Uncover and add the sesame oil. Stir and serve hot with a small dish of ground Szechuan pepper for guests to help themselves.

Note If you can't find Szechuan peppercorns, there is no real substitute for their flavour. However, you can easily obtain a peppery bite with regular peppercorns. Try a mixture of pink, green and black for a bit of variety, and add some freshly grated ginger to the stir-fry.

1 teaspoon Szechuan peppercorns, plus extra to serve

2 tablespoons peanut oil

4 spring onions/scallions, chopped

2 garlic cloves, sliced

1 small red bell pepper, deseeded and finely sliced lengthways

1 carrot, finely sliced lengthways into matchsticks

18 baby corn, each chopped into 3 pieces

freshly squeezed juice of ½ lemon

3–4 tablespoons dark soy sauce, or wheat-free tamari

1 small head of broccoli, broken into florets

14 sugar snap peas, trimmed

1 tablespoon toasted sesame oil

serves 4

This simple dish of South-east Asian flavours is a brilliant way to serve vegetables – spicy, barely cooked, but bathed in coconut milk. The recipe uses pattypan squash, sugarsnap peas and snake beans (also known as long beans) which keep their crunch better than ordinary beans, but you should use whichever crisp vegetables are in season. Fish sauce is used as a flavouring in many South-east Asian dishes, but vegetarian versions, based on soy beans, are available.

pattypan & snake beans in spicy coconut milk

500 ml/2 cups coconut milk

1 tablespoon vegetarian 'fish' sauce

1 tablespoon sugar

1 teaspoon dried chilli/hot pepper flakes (optional)

your choice of:

10 snake beans, cut into 5-cm/ 2-inch lengths

125 g/4½ oz. wing beans (available from Thai, Vietnamese or Chinese shops)

125 g/4½ oz. yellow and green pattypan squash halved lengthways

8 yellow or green mini courgettes/zucchini, halved lengthways

250 g/9 oz. sugar snap peas

8 ripe red or yellow cherry tomatoes, halved and deseeded

to serve

8 sprigs of fresh coriander/ cilantro

1 fresh red chilli, sliced

2 spring onions/scallions, sliced

serves 4

Fill a wok one-third full of salted water and heat until boiling. Add the snake beans and cook for 1 minute until blanched. Remove, drain and set aside. Repeat with the wing beans, pattypan squash and courgettes/zucchini.

Discard the water and add the coconut milk, fish sauce, sugar and chilli flakes (if using) and heat, stirring, to boiling point. Coconut milk must be stirred as it heats, or it will curdle: similarly, it should never be covered with a lid.

Add all the vegetables and simmer, stirring, for about 5 minutes until heated through. Transfer to a serving bowl, sprinkle with sprigs of coriander/cilantro, the sliced chilli and spring onions/scallions, and serve.

This is a hearty and flavoursome vegetarian dish traditionally eaten on the first day of Chinese New Year – Buddhists believe that meat should not be eaten on the first five days of the year. Every Buddhist family has their own version and ingredients vary from cook to cook. Vegetarian versions of oyster sauce are available from Asian stores and online.

buddha's delight

Combine all the sauce ingredients in a bowl and set aside.

Sprinkle the five-spice powder over the tofu.

Heat the oil in a wok or large frying pan until hot. Add the tofu to the wok in batches and stir-fry over high heat until golden all over. Remove the tofu from the wok and drain well on kitchen paper/paper towels.

Add the garlic to the wok and stir-fry for 1 minute, or until golden. Add the broccoli, bok choy, mangetout/snow peas, carrot and red pepper with a sprinkle of water and stir-fry over high heat for 2–3 minutes. Finally, throw in the water chestnuts and bamboo shoots.

Pour the sauce into the wok and bring to the boil, then reduce the heat and simmer gently for 2 minutes, or until the sauce has thickened. Divide between 4 bowls and serve with rice or noodles.

½ teaspoon Chinese five-spice

250 g/9 oz. firm tofu, cut into 2-cm/1-inch cubes

2 tablespoons vegetable oil

3 garlic cloves, crushed

200 g/7 oz. small broccoli florets

200 g/7 oz. miniature or baby bok choy, halved

200 g/7 oz. mangetout/snow peas

1 large carrot, cut into matchsticks

1 red bell pepper, deseeded and cut into matchsticks

85 g/3 oz. canned water chestnuts, drained and sliced

85 g/3 oz. canned sliced bamboo shoots, drained and rinsed

cooked rice or noodles, to serve

sauce

2 tablespoons vegetarian 'oyster' sauce

2 tablespoons light soy sauce

125 ml/½ cup vegetable stock

1 tablespoon cornflour/ cornstarch, combined with 2 tablespoons cold water

serves 4

Transform everyday vegetables into a memorable meal with a few carefully chosen whole and ground spices. As in many Indian-influenced dishes, a spiky ginger and garlic paste forms the basis of this stir-fry. Why not make extra and keep in the fridge or freezer for another day?

spiced mixed vegetables with cumin & fennel seeds

2.5-cm/1-inch piece of fresh ginger, peeled

2 garlic cloves, crushed

1 tablespoon vegetable oil

½ teaspoon fennel seeds

1 teaspoon cumin seeds

1 onion, halved and sliced

¼ teaspoon ground cumin

¼ teaspoon ground coriander

½ teaspoon chilli powder

150 g/5½ oz. canned chopped tomatoes

200 g/7 oz. cauliflower, cut into small florets

120 g/4½ oz. carrot, cut into 3-cm/1¼-inch matchsticks

120 g/4½ oz. trimmed green beans, cut on the diagonal into 3-cm/1¼-inch lengths

2 tablespoons chopped coriander/cilantro leaves, to garnish

sea salt

cooked rice, to serve

serves 2

Put the ginger and garlic in a pestle and mortar and grind until you have a rough paste. Alternatively, blitz in a food processor with a little water.

Heat the oil in a wok or large frying pan until hot. Add the fennel and cumin seeds and stir-fry over high heat until they start to pop. Add the onion and cook for a further 3–4 minutes, or until golden. Stir in the ginger and garlic paste and stir-fry for a further 2 minutes. Spoon in the ground cumin and coriander and the chilli powder, and after a few seconds, the canned tomatoes. Cook over high heat for 1 minute, or until most of the liquid has evaporated.

Throw the cauliflower and carrot into the wok with a good sprinkle of water, stir, then cover and cook for 2 minutes.

Add the beans, season with salt and cook for a further 2–3 minutes, uncovered, until the vegetables are cooked but still a little crunchy. Taste and add more salt if necessary.

Remove from the heat and stir in the chopped coriander/cilantro. Divide between 2 bowls and serve immediately with rice.

A dash of miso adds depth to this simple stir-fry, which is great for a light meal. You'll find edamame beans, also called soya beans, in the freezer section of the supermarket. They are high in protein and so make for a satisfying dish.

green vegetables with miso & sake

Combine all the sauce ingredients in a bowl and set aside.

Heat the oil in a wok or large frying pan until hot, then add the garlic and stir-fry over high heat for 30 seconds. Throw in the sugar snap peas and courgettes/zucchini and stir-fry for 2–3 minutes. Add the edamame beans and toss well, then pour in the sauce. Bring to the boil, then reduce the heat and simmer, stirring occasionally, for about 3 minutes, or until the vegetables are cooked through but still crunchy.

Taste and add a dash of soy sauce if you think it needs it. Divide between 4 bowls and serve immediately.

1 tablespoon vegetable oil

2 garlic cloves, crushed

200 g/7 oz. sugar snap peas

200 g/7 oz. baby courgettes/zucchini, chopped into chunks on the diagonal

200 g/7 oz. frozen edamame beans, defrosted

shoyu or tamari soy sauce, to taste (optional)

sauce

2 generous teaspoons red or brown miso paste

1 tablespoon mirin (Japanese rice wine)

1 tablespoon sake

150 ml/⅔ cup vegetable stock

1 tablespoon cornflour/cornstarch

serves 4

To lift your stir-fries out of the ordinary and into the sublime, you need to be a bit crafty with ingredients. Both lemongrass and kaffir lime leaves can be tricky to find, but they freeze well so keep a few stored in the freezer for quick meals such as this.

stir-fried asparagus, tofu & peppers with lemongrass, lime leaves & honey

1 tablespoon sunflower/safflower oil

50 g/1¾ oz. cashew nuts

2 large red chillies, sliced (and deseeded if you prefer it mild)

1 lemongrass stalk (outer layer discarded), finely minced

2 kaffir lime leaves, shredded

2 garlic cloves, peeled and crushed

2.5-cm/1-inch piece fresh ginger, unpeeled and sliced

250 g/9 oz. silken tofu, cubed

250 g/9 oz. medium asparagus tips

2 red bell peppers, cut into strips

1 tablespoon tamarind paste

2 tablespoons dark soy sauce

1 tablespoon clear honey

serves 4

Heat the oil in a wok or a large frying pan over medium/low heat and add the cashew nuts, chillies, lemongrass, lime leaves, garlic and ginger. Gently sauté for 1 minute.

Add the tofu, asparagus and red peppers and stir-fry for a further 2 minutes until they start to soften around the edges and the cashew nuts turn golden.

Pour in the tamarind paste, soy sauce and honey, along with 100 ml/½ cup water and turn up the heat to bring the liquid to the boil. Allow the contents of the wok to bubble up so that the liquid finishes cooking the vegetables and they are lovely and tender. This should take a further 3 minutes or so.

Transfer to bowls. Remove the slices of ginger, unless you particularly like hits of feisty ginger! Serve hot with steamed rice or egg noodles.

The great thing about stir-fries is that you can use almost any vegetable you like, as long as you cut them the same size so they cook evenly. Ginger adds a little warmth, but you can also experiment with different seasonings like Chinese five-spice, or if you like a bit of heat, add a little fresh or dried chilli.

stir-fry with vegetables & ginger

Heat the oils in a heavy-based frying pan or wok, then add the onion and fry for a few minutes until it looks soft and pale gold.

Add the courgette/zucchini, ginger, garlic and green beans to the pan and fry for another few minutes. Keep mixing everything so that it cooks evenly.

Add the soy sauce and continue to stir fry, tossing everything together.

Add the herbs and cooked noodles to the pan and stir through until nicely mixed.

Divide the stir-fry evenly between 4 bowls and serve immediately.

2 teaspoons sesame oil

2 teaspoons vegetable oil

1 onion, sliced

2 courgettes/zucchini, cut into matchsticks

2.5-cm/1-inch piece fresh ginger, grated

1 garlic clove, peeled and crushed

2 large handfuls of green beans

a little soy sauce

a large of handful fresh herbs such as parsley or mint, chopped

freshly cooked, hot egg noodles, to serve

serves 4

Pad Thai, probably the best-known of all Thai noodle dishes, takes only 5 minutes to cook. Use thick ribbon-like rice noodles ('rice sticks') for authenticity, or rice vermicelli or egg noodles. Tamarind, commonly used in Asian cooking, has a unique sour flavour, but you can substitute freshly squeezed lime juice.

pad thai

4 tablespoons sunflower/safflower oil

4 eggs, lightly beaten

150 g/5½ oz. dried thick rice noodles, soaked in warm water for 5 minutes, then drained

100 g/3½ oz. kale or other leafy green, tough central core removed and leaves coarsely chopped

4 tablespoons tamarind paste or 2 tablespoons freshly squeezed lime juice

4 tablespoons sweet chilli sauce

4 tablespoons light soy sauce

1 large carrot, about 200 g/7 oz., grated

100 g/3½ oz. beansprouts

to serve

50 g/1¾ oz. roasted peanuts, chopped

4 spring onions/scallions, finely sliced

fresh coriander/cilantro leaves, to garnish

serves 4

Heat a wok until very hot, then add the oil. Add the eggs and noodles and stir-fry for about 2 minutes, until the eggs are lightly scrambled.

Add the remaining ingredients and stir-fry for a further 3–5 minutes, until the noodles are cooked.

Divide between 4 warmed bowls and serve sprinkled with the peanuts, spring onions/scallions and coriander/cilantro.

casseroles & stews

This wonderful Italian vegetable casserole relies on using good-quality ingredients cooked to perfection. Its rustic simplicity allows the flavours of sweet, ripe peppers, meltingly soft potatoes and fruity olive oil to shine through.

calabrian-style potatoes & peppers

Heat the oil in a large, lidded frying pan. Add the red and yellow peppers and cook for 10 minutes, stirring occasionally, until starting to turn golden brown. Add the potatoes, salt and pepper to the pan, cover with a lid and cook for 5 minutes.

Remove the lid and continue cooking for 15 minutes, turning every few minutes as the potatoes begin to brown, taking care not to break them. If the potatoes start to stick, this will just add to the flavour of the dish, but don't let them burn.

When the potatoes are tender, transfer to a serving dish and top with the parsley, if using. Let cool for 5 minutes before serving.

150 ml/generous ½ cup olive oil

1 red bell pepper, halved, deseeded and thickly sliced

1 yellow bell pepper, halved, deseeded and thickly sliced

550 g/1¼ lbs. potatoes, thinly sliced

sea salt and freshly ground black pepper

a small bunch of flat leaf parsley, finely chopped, to serve (optional)

serves 4

This is a hearty hotpot packed with autumnal vegetables and rich with smoky paprika. Great northern beans are large and white, resembling butter/lima beans in shape but with a distinctive, delicate flavour. They are widely grown in Midwest America, where they are used in baked dishes. If you can't find them, butter/lima beans will do just as well.

smoky hotpot of great northern beans

100 g/½ cup dried great northern or butter/lima beans

2 tablespoons olive oil

1 large onion, chopped

2 garlic cloves, chopped

1 tablespoon capers, finely chopped

1 handful of fresh flat leaf parsley, chopped

2 teaspoons smoked Spanish paprika (pimentón)

1 celery stick, chopped

1 carrot, chopped

2 medium waxy potatoes, cut into 2.5-cm/1-inch dice

1 red bell pepper, chopped

500 ml/2 cups vegetable stock

sea salt and freshly ground black pepper

crusty bread, to serve

serves 4

Soak the dried beans in cold water for at least 6 hours or ideally overnight. Drain and put in a large saucepan with sufficient just-boiled water to cover. Cook for 30 minutes until softened. Drain and set aside until needed.

Put the oil in a saucepan set over medium heat. Add the onion and cook for 4–5 minutes until softened. Add the garlic, capers, parsley and paprika to the pan and stir-fry for 2 minutes. Add the celery, carrot, potatoes and red pepper and cook for 2 minutes, stirring constantly to coat the vegetables in the flavoured oil.

Add the stock and beans and bring to the boil. Reduce the heat and partially cover the pan with a lid. Let simmer for 40 minutes, stirring often, until all the vegetables are cooked. Season to taste and serve with bread for dipping in the sauce.

This Spanish vegetable sauté (known as Pisto Manchego) is probably based on an earlier Moorish dish. The original didn't include tomatoes or peppers, because these weren't introduced from the New World until the 16th century, after the expulsion of the Moors. This dish is very good eaten cold or served warm with a hot poached egg on top, or with a plate of fried bread.

vegetable sauté

Heat half the oil in a heavy saucepan, add the onions and garlic and fry over medium heat for 5 minutes until softened. Remove to a bowl. Increase the heat, add the remaining oil, cumin and aubergine/eggplant, stir until they take up the oil and soften slightly, then add the tomatoes and their juices. Simmer until the mixture starts to thicken.

Fold in the courgettes/zucchini, peppers and chopped oregano, season with salt and pepper and simmer gently, uncovered, until soft. Fold in the vinegar and serve hot or cold with the oregano leaves sprinkled over.

150 ml/generous ½ cup extra virgin olive oil

2 onions, chopped

4 garlic cloves, finely chopped

½ teaspoon cumin seeds

2 medium aubergines/eggplants, chopped into 1-cm/½-inch cubes

6 tomatoes, skinned, deseeded and chopped, with the juices reserved

300 g/10½ oz. courgettes/zucchini, cut into 1-cm/½-inch cubes

3 large roasted red bell peppers from a jar, cut into 1-cm/½-inch cubes

1 tablespoon coarsely chopped fresh oregano, plus extra leaves to serve

2 teaspoons sherry vinegar or red wine vinegar

sea salt and freshly ground black pepper

serves 4–6

This dish falls somewhere between a stew and a soup: to make use of the abundant sauce, serve with fragrant jasmine rice. If you like things spicy, add two chillies and all their seeds; if not, add one and keep the seeds out. It will be very mild and the specks of red are pretty against the orange.

sweet potato, spinach & chickpea stew with coconut

1 tablespoon vegetable oil

1 onion, halved and sliced

30-g/1-oz. piece of fresh ginger, peeled and grated

1–2 fresh red chillies, halved and sliced

1 teaspoon curry powder

1 teaspoon ground cumin

1.3 kg/3 lbs. sweet potatoes, peeled and cubed

400-ml/14-oz. can coconut milk

450 ml/1¾ cups vegetable stock

410-g/14-oz. can chickpeas, drained

225 g/8 oz. fresh baby spinach leaves, washed

sea salt

jasmine rice, to serve

serves 4–6

Heat the oil in a large saucepan. Add the onion and cook over low heat for 3–5 minutes, until just soft. Add the ginger, chillies, curry powder, cumin and a pinch of salt. Cook for 1–2 minutes, stirring, until aromatic.

Add the sweet potatoes and stir to coat in the spices. Add the coconut milk and stock and a little water if necessary, just to cover the sweet potatoes; the mixture should be soupy as it will cook down. Add a little salt, bring to the boil, then simmer, uncovered, for 15 minutes.

Add the chickpeas and continue to simmer for 15–20 minutes more, until the sweet potatoes are tender.

Add the spinach, in batches, stirring to blend and waiting for each batch to wilt before adding the next. Taste and adjust the seasoning if necessary. Serve immediately with jasmine rice.

For nights when you want dinner in a hurry, this delicious stroganoff can be on the table in just 10 minutes. Serve with basmati and wild rice or couscous, together with some green beans or cabbage.

mustardy mushroom stroganoff

Cook the onion in a covered saucepan with 3 tablespoons of the stock for about 4 minutes or until softened and the liquid has evaporated. Stir in the mushrooms, garlic and seasoning, then add the remaining stock, mustard and tomato purée/paste.

Cook, covered, for 2 minutes, then remove the lid and cook rapidly for 2 minutes to reduce the liquid to a syrup. Stir in the crème fraîche and parsley and serve immediately on a bed of rice or couscous.

½ small onion, sliced

150 ml/generous ½ cup vegetable stock

150 g/5½ oz. mixed mushrooms, chopped if large

1 garlic clove, crushed

1 teaspoon wholegrain mustard

½ teaspoon tomato purée/paste

1 tablespoon crème fraîche

chopped fresh parsley, to serve

sea salt and freshly ground black pepper

serves 1

Any kind of olive can be used here but if you can find some marinated with whole coriander seeds, these are the best ones to use. This is a summer stew and is best eaten lukewarm or at room temperature. Serve with a salad made from cos lettuce dressed with extra virgin olive oil and lemon juice, some feta and crusty bread.

greek summer vegetable stew with lemon & olives

2 tablespoons olive oil

1 onion, chopped

500 g/1 lb. small new potatoes (red if available), cubed

350 g/12 oz. courgettes/zucchini, halved and quartered lengthways, then sliced thickly

3 garlic cloves, sliced

¼ teaspoon paprika

¼ teaspoon cayenne pepper

2 x 400-g/14-oz. cans chopped tomatoes

leaves from a small bunch of fresh parsley, finely chopped

sprigs from a small bunch of fresh dill, finely chopped

250 g/9 oz. fine green beans, halved

100 g/¾ cup pitted cracked green olives

freshly squeezed juice of ½ lemon

sea salt and freshly ground black pepper

serves 4–6

Heat the oil in a large saucepan. Add the onion and cook over low heat for 3–5 minutes, until soft. Add the potatoes, courgettes/zucchini, garlic, paprika, cayenne and a pinch of salt and cook, stirring to coat in the oil, for 1 minute.

Add the tomatoes, parsley and half the dill. Stir to combine and add some water to thin slightly; about 125 ml/½ cup should be enough. Season well, then cover and simmer for 30 minutes.

Add the beans, cover and continue to simmer for about 20 minutes more, until the beans are tender. Stir in the olives, lemon juice and remaining dill. Taste and adjust the seasoning if necessary. Serve at room temperature with a simple salad of cos lettuce, some feta cheese and plenty of crusty bread.

Although this ratatouille is unashamedly olive-oil laden, it shouldn't be greasy, which is difficult as aubergine/eggplant tends to soak up oil like a sponge. Microwaving them prior to frying can help keep oil absorption to a minimum. If you don't have a microwave, light steaming will have the same effect. Serve with rice and a little grated cheese for a satisfying meal.

ratatouille

Put the aubergine/eggplant cubes in a microwave-proof bowl with 3 tablespoons water and microwave on high for 6 minutes. Drain and set aside.

Heat 3 tablespoons of the oil in a large saucepan. Add the onions and cook over low heat for 3–5 minutes, until soft. Season with a little salt.

Add the bell peppers and cook for a further 5–8 minutes, stirring occasionally. Season with a little salt.

Add 1 more tablespoon of the oil and then the courgettes/zucchini. Mix well and cook for 5 minutes more. Season with a little more salt.

Add 2 more tablespoons of the oil and the drained aubergines/eggplant. Cook, stirring often, for a further 5 minutes. Add the tomatoes, 5 of the garlic cloves, half of the basil and 1 more tablespoon of the oil, if required. Check the seasoning and adjust if necessary. Cook for 5 minutes. Cover, reduce the heat and simmer gently for 30 minutes, stirring occasionally.

Stir in the remaining garlic and basil just before serving. Serve with rice or crusty bread, as preferred.

1 kg/2¼ lbs. aubergines/eggplant, cut into cubes

6–7 tablespoons olive oil

2 onions, coarsely chopped

2 red bell peppers, halved, deseeded and cut into pieces

2 yellow bell peppers, halved, deseeded and cut into pieces

1 green bell pepper, halved, deseeded and cut into pieces

750 g/1½ lbs. courgettes/zucchini, halved lengthways and sliced

6 fresh plum tomatoes, halved, deseeded and chopped

6 garlic cloves, crushed

a large handful of fresh basil leaves, coarsely chopped

sea salt and freshly ground black pepper

rice, to serve (optional)

serves 4–6

With its lush, intriguing taste, okra is the beloved vegetable of the Eastern Mediterranean. This dish can be cooked well in advance and will wait happily at the table. The dried limes, which can be obtained from Arab or Indian stores, add an altogether new dimension to its sweet taste.

okra with dried limes

800 g/2 lbs. fresh okra

150 ml/⅔ cup extra virgin olive oil

1 large onion, sliced

1 teaspoon ground coriander

½ teaspoon ground allspice

700 g/1¾ lbs. fresh tomatoes, sliced, or 400 g/14 oz canned tomatoes

2 dried limes (optional)

½ teaspoon sugar

2 tablespoons finely chopped fresh coriander/cilantro

sea salt and freshly ground black pepper

serves 6

To prepare the okra, pare the conical tops with a sharp knife (similar to peeling potatoes). Put in a bowl, cover with cold water briefly, then drain – handle with care.

Heat the oil in a wide saucepan, add the onion and sauté until light golden. Add the ground coriander and allspice, then when aromatic, add the tomatoes, dried limes, if using, sugar, salt and pepper. Cook for 10 minutes, pressing the limes with a spatula to extract their juices.

Add the okra and spread them evenly in the pan. Add enough hot water until they are almost immersed in the sauce.

Cook gently for about 30 minutes – shake the pan occasionally but don't stir as okra is fragile. Sprinkle the fresh coriander/cilantro over the top and simmer for a further 5–10 minutes. Serve warm or at room temperature.

Although it may sound unusual, chocolate is the secret
ingredient of this Mexican-inspired dish. It adds a
wonderfully rich, intense flavour to the vegetables.
It is delicious served with boiled rice or chilli cornbread.

quick vegetarian mole

Heat the oil in a saucepan and fry the onion, pepper, garlic and spices
for 5 minutes. Add the sweet potatoes, canned tomatoes, beans,
chilli sauce and 300 ml/1¼ cups water and bring to the boil. Cover
and simmer over gentle heat for 30 minutes.

Stir in the chocolate and fresh coriander/cilantro and cook for a final
5 minutes. Taste and adjust the seasoning, then serve.

2 tablespoons peanut or
sunflower/safflower oil

1 red onion, chopped

1 large red bell pepper, deseeded
and chopped

2 garlic cloves

2 teaspoons ground coriander

1 teaspoon ground cumin

½ teaspoon ground cinnamon

400 g/1 lb. sweet potatoes, cut
into cubes

400-g/14-oz. can chopped
tomatoes

400-g/14-oz. can red kidney
beans, rinsed and drained

1–2 teaspoons chilli sauce

25 g/1 oz. dark chocolate, grated

2 tablespoons chopped fresh
coriander/cilantro

sea salt and freshly ground
black pepper

serves 4

So many potato recipes are baked or roasted, but it's nice to have a simple stovetop preparation. This one is a lovely, autumnal dish that is quick to throw together, so perfect for a midweek supper, just the thing when days and nights are getting cooler. Chanterelles are a favourite mushroom, but any kind can be used here, including dried mushrooms, but these will need to be soaked in warm water beforehand.

wild mushroom & potato ragout with leek

1 kg/2¼ lbs. new potatoes

2 tablespoons olive oil

1 onion, halved and sliced

1 trimmed leek, thinly sliced into rounds

2 tablespoons unsalted butter

300 g/10½ oz. chanterelle mushrooms, cut into bite-sized pieces

2 garlic cloves, crushed

1 teaspoon dried thyme

400 ml/1⅔ cups vegetable stock

1 bay leaf

2 tablespoons crème fraîche or sour cream

a large handful of fresh flat leaf parsley leaves, chopped

sea salt and freshly ground black pepper

serves 4

Put the potatoes in a large saucepan with sufficient water to cover. Add a pinch of salt and bring to the boil. Cook until tender when pierced with a knife. When cool enough to handle, cut into large dice.

Heat the oil in a large saucepan and add the onion and leek. Season lightly and cook over medium heat for 2–3 minutes, until soft.

Add the butter and stir until melted. Add the mushrooms, garlic and thyme. Cook, stirring, for 1–2 minutes. Season lightly, then add the stock, bay leaf and cooked potatoes. Add a little water to just cover if necessary.

Simmer, uncovered, for 30–40 minutes, until the liquid has reduced by half. Taste and adjust the seasoning if necessary. Stir in the crème fraîche and parsley and serve immediately.

The vegetarian recipes you find in Indian cuisine are some of the most delicious in the world as they embrace the philosophy of cooking fresh produce at its best, keeping it simple and letting the flavours speak for themselves. This is a spicy treat that's perfect if you like things hot.

spiced cauliflower with red pepper & peas

Put the cauliflower florets in a large bowl with the cumin and turmeric and toss until evenly coated in the spices.

Put the oil in a frying pan set over medium/high heat. Add the cauliflower, mustard seeds and curry leaves and cook for 8–10 minutes, turning the pieces often so that they soften and colour with the spices. Add the onion and red pepper and cook for 5 minutes. Add the ginger, garlic and chilli and stir-fry for 1 minute, then add the stock, tomatoes and peas. Reduce the heat and let simmer gently for 10 minutes until the vegetables are tender and cooked through.

Spoon over basmati rice to serve, if liked.

½ head of cauliflower, cut into large florets

2 teaspoons ground cumin

1 teaspoon ground turmeric

3 tablespoons light olive oil

2 teaspoons black mustard seeds

6–8 curry leaves

1 onion, sliced

1 small red bell pepper, thinly sliced

1 tablespoon finely grated fresh ginger

2 garlic cloves, chopped

1 large green chilli, sliced

125 ml/½ cup vegetable stock

2 ripe tomatoes, chopped

125 g/1 cup freshly shelled peas

steamed or boiled basmati rice, to serve (optional)

serves 4

Similar to a French ratatouille, this delicious dish is spiked with a touch of ras-el-hanout* and sweetened with succulent dates. Serve it as a main course, with fresh crusty bread, or as an accompaniment to a tagine.

moroccan ratatouille with dates

4–5 tablespoons olive oil

1 onion, halved lengthways and sliced crossways

2 garlic cloves, chopped

1 red bell pepper, deseeded and halved lengthways and sliced crossways

1 aubergine/eggplant, halved lengthways and sliced crossways

2 courgettes/zucchini, sliced

225 g/8 oz. ready-to-eat pitted dates, halved lengthways

2 x 400-g/14-oz. cans chopped tomatoes

2 teaspoons ras-el-hanout

1–2 teaspoons sugar

leaves from a small bunch of fresh flat leaf parsley, coarsely chopped

sea salt and freshly ground black pepper

serves 4–6

Heat the oil in a tagine or a heavy-based casserole. Add the onion and garlic and cook for 2–3 minutes until they begin to soften.

Add the pepper, aubergine/eggplant and courgettes/zucchini and cook for a further 3–4 minutes. Add the dates, tomatoes, ras-el-hanout and sugar and mix thoroughly. Cover and cook for about 40 minutes, until the vegetables are tender.

Season to taste with salt and pepper and sprinkle the chopped parsley over the top.

*Note Ras-el-hanout is a spice mixture mostly identified with Moroccan cooking, but is also found in other parts of North Africa. The name literally means 'top of the store' as each spice vendor would have their own unique recipe. The spices usually include: cinnamon, saffron pepper, cardamom, nutmeg, ginger and coriander. It is widely available from supermarkets and specialist online retailers.

The term Napolitana is used here to loosely describe the predominance of tomatoes in this Mediterranean-style stew although the flavours could easily be described as Greek, given the inclusion of fresh oregano and feta. There are few ingredients in this dish, so the tomatoes must be of premium quality and vine-ripened in the summer sun.

napolitana lentil stew

Put the lentils in a large saucepan, add sufficient cold water to cover and set over high heat. Bring to the boil, then reduce the heat and let simmer for 20 minutes until the lentils are tender but retain a little 'bite'. Drain and set aside until needed.

Put the oil in a saucepan set over high heat. Add the onion, garlic, oregano and chilli/hot pepper flakes and cook for 5 minutes, stirring often, until the onion softens. Add the capers, tomatoes, passata, lentils and 250 ml/1 cup water. Bring to the boil, then reduce the heat and let simmer gently for 10 minutes, stirring occasionally.

Spoon into warmed serving dishes, top with the olives and feta and serve with crusty bread on the side for dipping into the rich sauce.

100 g/½ cup green or brown lentils

3 tablespoons olive oil

1 onion, chopped

2 garlic cloves, chopped

1 small handful of fresh oregano, chopped

1 teaspoon dried chilli/hot pepper flakes

1½ tablespoons salted capers, rinsed

2 ripe tomatoes, roughly chopped

250 ml/1 cup passata/strained tomatoes

60 g/2 oz. small black olives

100 g/4 oz. vegetarian feta cheese (see note on page 4), crumbled

crusty bread, to serve

serves 4

bakes & gratins

A classic of French home cooking, this gratin includes a topping of tangy goats' cheese. If you grow your own herbs, add whatever is on offer: savory, marjoram, oregano or any other soft-leaved herb, the more the merrier. This is perfect, simply served with a few ripe tomatoes and a big basket of fresh crusty bread.

courgette gratin with fresh herbs & goats' cheese

Preheat the oven to 190°C (375°F) Gas 5.

Put the cream, parsley, chives, nutmeg, salt and pepper in a small bowl and whisk together. Add half the Gruyère.

Arrange half the courgette/zucchini slices in the prepared baking dish, sprinkle with the remaining Gruyère and season with a little salt. Top with the remaining courgette/zucchini slices, season again and pour over the cream mixture. Crumble the goats' cheese over the top.

Bake in the preheated oven for 35–45 minutes, until browned. Serve immediately with a mixed salad and plenty of crusty bread.

Variation If preferred, you can make the gratin in 4 individual dishes: simply reduce the cooking time by about 5–10 minutes.

250 ml/1 cup double/heavy cream

leaves from a small bunch of fresh flat leaf parsley, finely chopped

a small bunch of chives, snipped

a pinch of freshly grated nutmeg

75 g/2½ oz. vegetarian Gruyère cheese (see note on page 4), grated

1.5 kg/3½ lbs. courgettes/ zucchini, very thinly sliced

150 g/5½ oz. soft goats' cheese

sea salt and freshly ground black pepper

a 24-cm/10-inch round, deep-sided baking dish, well buttered

serves 4

Courgettes/zucchini are much more flavourful when cooked this way – bathed in garlic and olive oil, then stuffed with sweet, ripe cherry tomatoes and enveloped in melting fontina cheese. Delightfully fresh and summery.

mediterranean vegetables baked with fontina

6 medium courgettes/zucchini (as straight as possible)

2 garlic cloves, chopped

2 tablespoons olive oil, plus extra for sprinkling

about 30 cherry tomatoes, halved

3–4 tablespoons dried breadcrumbs

250 g/9 oz. vegetarian fontina cheese (see note on page 4), sliced

sea salt and freshly ground black pepper

a shallow ovenproof dish, greased

serves 6

Preheat the oven to 160°C (325°F) Gas 3.

Halve the courgettes/zucchini lengthways and trim a little off the uncut sides so that they will sit still like boats. Using a teaspoon, scoop out the soft-seeded centres. Arrange the boats in a row in the prepared baking dish.

Put the garlic, olive oil, salt and pepper in a bowl, stir well, then brush over the cut surfaces of the courgettes/zucchini. Arrange the halved tomatoes in the grooves. Season well, then sprinkle with olive oil and breadcrumbs. Bake in the preheated oven for 30 minutes.

Carefully remove from the oven and arrange the sliced fontina over the courgettes/zucchini and tomatoes. Return the dish to the oven for another 10 minutes to melt the cheese. Serve immediately while the cheese is still bubbling.

Baking sliced potatoes and mushrooms in layers allows the potatoes to absorb the juices and earthy flavour of the mushrooms. Try to use the darkest mushrooms you can find – they will have the best taste. For a more intense flavour, try mixing fresh ones with reconstituted dried mushrooms.

potato & mushroom gratin

Preheat the oven to 180°C (350°F) Gas 4.

Peel the potatoes and slice thickly, putting them in a bowl of cold water as you go. Trim the mushrooms and slice thickly. Put half the potatoes in a layer in the bottom of the dish, sprinkle with olive oil and cover with half the mushrooms.

Put the breadcrumbs, cheese, parsley, salt and pepper in a bowl and mix well. Spread half this mixture over the mushrooms, then sprinkle with more olive oil. Cover with a layer of the remaining potatoes, then a layer of the remaining mushrooms. Finally, sprinkle with the remaining breadcrumb mixture and more oil.

Cover with foil and bake in the preheated oven for 30 minutes. Uncover and cook for a further 30 minutes until the potatoes are tender and the top is golden brown.

Note If you blanch the potato slices first for 5 minutes in boiling salted water, they will take only 30 minutes to cook.

1 kg/2 lbs. medium potatoes

750 g/1¾ lbs. flavoursome mushrooms such as dark flat cap, chestnut or portobello (or use fresh wild mushrooms)

extra virgin olive oil, for sprinkling

175 g/6 oz. stale (not dry) white breadcrumbs

4 tablespoons freshly grated Parmesan-style cheese (see note on page 4)

4 tablespoons chopped fresh flat leaf parsley

sea salt and freshly ground black pepper

a deep gratin or other ovenproof dish

serves 4

A pretty Italian gratin bursting with flavour – and a satisfying meal in itself. Juicy, sweet tomato halves are baked with briefly fried, thinly sliced aubergines/eggplant and freshly grated Parmesan-style hard cheese. Delicious.

parmigiana di melanzane

1 large aubergine/eggplant

500 g/1 lb. very ripe, red tomatoes

about 150 ml/⅔ cup olive oil

4 tablespoons freshly chopped basil

125 g/4½ oz. freshly grated Parmesan-style cheese (see note on page 4)

sea salt and freshly ground black pepper

a shallow ovenproof dish, well buttered

serves 4

Preheat the oven to 200°C (400°F) Gas 6.

Cut the aubergine/eggplant lengthways into 5-mm/¼-inch thick slices. Sprinkle with salt and let drain in a colander for 30 minutes. Rinse well and pat dry with kitchen paper. Cut the tomatoes in half.

Heat the oil in a frying pan and fry the aubergines/eggplant in batches until deep golden brown. Drain on kitchen paper. Arrange a layer of aubergines in the prepared dish, then top with a layer of tomato halves, cut side up. Sprinkle with the chopped basil, salt, pepper and half the cheese. Add another layer of aubergines/eggplant, then sprinkle with the remaining cheese.

Bake in the preheated oven for 20–25 minutes, or until browned and bubbling on top. Let cool slightly and serve warm, or cool completely and serve as a salad.

Long, thin, sweet Romano peppers are best for this dish. However, if they aren't in season, ordinary peppers can be used, though a little extra filling may be needed, as they tend to be larger.

stuffed peppers

Preheat the oven to 180°C (350°F) Gas 4.

Put the pepper halves skin side down onto the oiled baking sheet.

Put the mushrooms, mozzarella, garlic, oil, olives and paprika into a bowl. Add salt and pepper to taste and mix well. Spoon the mixture into the peppers. Cook near the top of the preheated oven for 30 minutes. Serve hot or warm.

4 long bell peppers, halved lengthways, cored and deseeded

200 g/7 oz. mushrooms, coarsely chopped

150 g/5½ oz. vegetarian mozzarella cheese (see note on page 4), drained and cut into large dice

2 garlic cloves, crushed and chopped

3 tablespoons olive oil

75 g/2½ oz. pitted olives, chopped

½ tablespoon paprika

sea salt and freshly ground black pepper

a baking sheet, lightly oiled

serves 4

This is really rich and ideally served with some crusty bread or a simple green salad with a tangy vinaigrette. It is also a great brunch dish, perfect with poached eggs and hot buttered toast.

baked spinach mornay

3 tablespoons butter

2 tablespoons plain/all-purpose flour

750 ml/3 cups whole milk

200 g/7 oz. vegetarian fontina cheese (see note on page 4), cubed

1 onion, chopped

1 garlic clove, chopped

1 kg/2 lbs. fresh spinach leaves, chopped

¼ teaspoon freshly grated nutmeg

toasted and buttered sourdough bread, to serve (optional)

serves 6

Preheat the oven to 180°C (350°F) Gas 4.

Put 2 tablespoons of the butter in a saucepan set over medium heat. When it is melted and sizzling, add the flour and cook for 1 minute, stirring constantly, until a thick paste forms.

Reduce the heat to low and slowly pour the milk into the pan, whisking constantly, until all the milk is incorporated and the mixture is smooth and lump-free. Add the cheese and stir until it has melted into the sauce. Set aside until needed.

Heat the remaining butter in a large frying pan set over high heat, add the onion and garlic and cook for 2–3 minutes, until the onion has softened. Add the spinach, cover with a lid, and cook for 4–5 minutes, stirring often, until the spinach has wilted. Transfer the spinach to a large bowl. Pour in the cheese sauce and stir to combine. Spoon the mixture into a large baking dish.

Sprinkle the nutmeg over the top and bake in the preheated oven for 30 minutes until the top of the mornay is golden and bubbling. Serve on slices of toasted and buttered sourdough bread, if liked.

This comforting gratin is cooked under the grill/broiler, so is far quicker to prepare then oven-baked gratins. You may be tempted to discard the fleshy white central ribs of chard leaves but they make a delicate-tasting gratin.

chard, onion & cheese gratin

Heat a saucepan, add the oil and 1 tablespoon of the butter, and tip in the onion. Cover with a lid and cook over low heat for about 5–6 minutes until beginning to soften. Stir in the thyme, then add the chard stalks and cook for another 3–4 minutes. Season.

Preheat the grill/broiler.

Stir in the flour, then add the milk, bring to the boil, and simmer until the sauce has thickened. Stir in the chard leaves and cook for 1 minute, then add the crème fraîche and cheese. Tip into the ovenproof dish. Mix the remaining 3 tablespoons cheese with the breadcrumbs, if using, and scatter over the gratin. Chop the remaining butter into little pieces and dot over the top. Grill/broil until brown and bubbling.

1 tablespoon olive oil

2 tablespoons butter

1 medium/large onion, roughly chopped

1 teaspoon finely chopped fresh thyme leaves or ½ teaspoon dried thyme

stalks from a large bunch of chard, washed, trimmed, and sliced, plus 4 chard leaves, roughly shredded

1 tablespoon plain/all-purpose flour

150 ml/⅔ cup whole milk

1 tablespoon crème fraîche or double/heavy cream (optional)

30 g/⅓ cup freshly grated Parmesan-style cheese, plus 3 tablespoons for the topping (see note on page 4)

2 tablespoons fresh breadcrumbs (optional)

sea salt and freshly ground black pepper

a medium ovenproof dish

serves 2

This rich, creamy, garlicky sauce is offset by the earthy flavours of root vegetables, plus the slightly tart and highly aromatic sage. It is incredibly straightforward to prepare. Serve with a herby leaf salad with mustard dressing.

roasted vegetable dauphinois

1 garlic clove

butter, for brushing

400 g/14 oz. parsnips, topped, tailed and cut into 1-cm/½-inch diagonal slices

1 handful of fresh sage leaves

350 g/12 oz. carrots, cut into 1-cm/½-inch diagonal slices

350 g/12 oz. uncooked beetroot, scrubbed well and cut into 1-cm/½-inch diagonal slices

275 ml/1 generous cup double/heavy cream

1 tablespoon olive oil

sea salt and freshly ground black pepper

a baking dish, about 30 cm/ 12 inches square

serves 4

Preheat the oven to 200°C (400°F) Gas 6.

Rub the garlic around the base and sides of the baking dish, then brush with butter. Pack overlapping slices of parsnips into the dish. Season well with salt and pepper, then add one-third of the sage leaves.

Repeat the process, first with the carrots, then the beetroot, seasoning each layer with salt and pepper and dotting with the remaining sage. Pour in the cream.

Cover the dish with foil and bake in the preheated oven for 1 hour 40 minutes. Remove the foil and lightly sprinkle the top with the olive oil. Return to the oven and continue cooking for a further 20 minutes or until the vegetables are very tender.

This is a very simple dish, very impressive and hugely delightful. Although the thought of peeling and slicing so many vegetables may be a little off-putting, the wonderful smells emanating from the oven once it is all done will make it well worth the effort.

root vegetable gratin

Preheat the oven to 200°C (400°F) Gas 6.

Put all the vegetable slices in a large bowl and toss gently to combine. Set aside.

Combine the cream, crème fraîche and milk in a small saucepan and heat just to melt the crème fraîche. Stir well and season.

Arrange half of the vegetable slices in the prepared baking dish. Sprinkle with a little salt and one-third of the cheese. Pour over one-third of the cream mixture. Top with the rest of the vegetable slices, the remaining cheese and a sprinkle of salt. Pour over the remaining cream mixture and bake in the preheated oven for 1–1½ hours, until browned on top. Serve immediately.

3 small turnips (about 375 g/ 13 oz.), peeled, halved and very thinly sliced

½ a celeriac (about 325 g/11 oz.), peeled, halved and very thinly sliced

½ a swede/rutabaga (about 450 g/1 lb.), peeled, halved and very thinly sliced

650 g/1½ lbs. waxy potatoes, peeled, halved and very thinly sliced

225 ml/1 scant cup double/heavy cream

6 tablespoons crème fraîche

250 ml/1 cup milk

125 g/1½ cups grated vegetarian Cheddar cheese

sea salt and freshly ground black pepper

a 30 x 20-cm/12 x 8-inch baking dish, very well buttered

serves 4–6

This gratin reheats well, so make it in advance to be sure it is perfectly cooked. A time-saving trick is to cover the dish and microwave on high for 10 minutes, then finish it off in the oven for 45 minutes.

potatoes dauphinoise

1 kg/2 lbs. waxy potatoes (Desirée are good), peeled and thinly sliced

125 g/1¼ cups freshly grated Parmesan-style cheese (see note on page 4)

freshly grated nutmeg

300 ml/1¼ cups double/heavy cream

sea salt and freshly ground black pepper

a shallow ovenproof dish, very well buttered

serves 6

Preheat the oven to 160°C (325°F) Gas 3.

Layer the potatoes in the dish, seasoning each layer with cheese, nutmeg, salt and pepper. Pour over the cream and sprinkle any remaining cheese over the top.

If the dish will stand it, set it on top of the stove and lightly warm through before baking in the preheated oven for about 1 hour or until the potatoes are tender and the top is golden and crisp.

This hearty, rustic dish just shows how good the simple things can be. Ripe, juicy tomatoes and peppers, drizzled with a splash of good olive oil and with whole garlic cloves and thyme sprigs result in wonderfully caramelized slow-roasted veggies. With the addition of some chickpeas, to soak up the flavours, this is a perfect autumn dish.

roasted early autumn vegetables with chickpeas

Preheat the oven to 180°C (350°F) Gas 4. Put the mushrooms, tomatoes, red and yellow peppers, onion, fennel and garlic in a large roasting tray. Sprinkle the salt evenly over the vegetables and drizzle with the oil. Roast in the preheated oven for 1 hour.

Remove the tray from the oven and turn the vegetables. Add the chickpeas and thyme sprigs. Return the tray to the oven and roast for a further 30 minutes, until the edges of the vegetables are just starting to blacken and char. Serve hot or warm.

12 small mushrooms

2 ripe tomatoes, halved

1 red bell pepper, cut into strips

1 yellow bell pepper, cut into strips

1 red onion, cut into wedges

1 small fennel bulb, sliced into thin wedges

1 garlic bulb, broken into individual cloves but left unpeeled

2 teaspoons sea salt

2 tablespoons olive oil

400-g/14-oz. can chickpeas, drained and rinsed

2 fresh thyme or rosemary sprigs

serves 4

A simplified version of that old-time favourite, macaroni cheese, but with creamy mascarpone as the sauce base there is no need for flour and no risk of unappetizing lumps!

three-cheese baked penne

350 g/12 oz. dried pasta, such as penne

400 g/14 oz. mascarpone cheese

2 tablespoons wholegrain mustard

300 g/10½ oz. vegetarian fontina cheese (see note on page 4), grated

4 tablespoons freshly grated Parmesan-style cheese (see note on page 4)

salt and freshly ground black pepper

a baking dish, about 30 x 20 cm/ 30 x 8 inches

serves 4

Preheat the oven to 200°C (400°F) Gas 6.

Bring a large saucepan of water to the boil. Add a good pinch of salt, then the pasta, and cook until al dente, or according to the timings on the packet.

Drain the pasta well and return it to the warm pan. Add the mascarpone and stir to mix. Add the mustard, fontina and Parmesan-style cheese, with salt and pepper to taste. Stir to mix.

Transfer to the baking dish and cook in the preheated oven for 25–30 minutes until golden and bubbling.

rice & grains

This technique of cooking rice is Middle Eastern in origin, but has spread far and wide – similar rice dishes can be found in European, Asian, Latin American, Caribbean and Indian cuisines, and it is known by many names including pilaf, pilav and pulao.

orange vegetable pilau

Put the oil in a heavy-based saucepan set over high heat. Add the onion, garlic, ginger and chilli and cook for 5 minutes, stirring often. Add the spices and almonds and cook for a further 5 minutes, until the spices become aromatic and look very dark in the pan.

Add the rice and cook for a minute, stirring well to coat the rice in the spices. Add the carrot, pumpkin and sweet potato to the pan. Pour in 600 ml/2½ cups water and stir well, loosening any grains of rice that are stuck to the bottom. Bring to the boil, then reduce the heat to low, cover with a tight-fitting lid and cook for 25 minutes, stirring occasionally.

Add the lime juice and coriander/cilantro, stir well to combine and serve.

2 tablespoons light olive oil

1 onion, chopped

2 garlic cloves, chopped

1 tablespoon finely grated fresh ginger

1 large red chilli, finely chopped

1 teaspoon ground coriander

1 teaspoon ground cumin

1 teaspoon turmeric

50 g/½ cup flaked/slivered almonds

300 g/1½ cups basmati rice

1 carrot, cut into large chunks

200 g/7 oz. pumpkin or squash, peeled, deseeded and cut into wedges

1 small sweet potato, peeled and cut into thick half-circles

freshly squeezed juice of 1 lime

1 handful of fresh coriander/ cilantro leaves, chopped

serves 4

This vegetarian dish comes from Valencia, where it is served during the Lenten fast. Its Spanish name – *arroz al horno con perdiz* – means 'with partridge', though the partridge is really a whole bulb of garlic.

baked rice with garlic

100 ml/½ cup olive oil

1 whole bulb of garlic

1 large onion, finely chopped

4 tomatoes, skinned, deseeded and chopped (keep the juices)

1 teaspoon sweet paprika (pimentón dulce)

350 g/1¾ cups round-grain rice, such as bomba or Calasparra

up to 1 litre/4 cups vegetable stock or water

400-g/14-oz. can chickpeas, rinsed and drained

50 g/⅓ cup raisins, soaked in hot water for 30 minutes until plump

sea salt and freshly ground black pepper

a paella pan, cazuela or other ovenproof pan, 20–25 cm/ 8–10 inches diameter

serves 6

Preheat the oven to 180°C (350°F) Gas 4.

Heat the oil in a paella pan, heatproof cazuela, heatproof shallow casserole or a frying pan with ovenproof handle. Add the garlic head and onion and fry for 12 minutes over low heat until the garlic is pale golden and beginning to soften and the onion soft and golden.

Remove the garlic and reserve. Increase the heat and add the tomatoes and juices. Cook until the mixture starts to thicken a little. Stir in the paprika, salt and pepper.

Stir in the rice. Add half the stock or water and bring slowly to the boil. Add the chickpeas, drain the raisins and gently fold them into the rice. Put the garlic in the centre and bake in the preheated oven for 10 minutes. Heat the remaining stock or water, then add as much as the rice seems to need. Continue baking for 10–15 minutes before serving, covering the top with foil if it seems to be over-browning or drying out. Serve from the pan.

This delicious Indian-style pilau is a healthy and satisfying one-pot dish. Serve it with a spoonful of low-fat natural yogurt and some chopped fresh coriander/cilantro, which acts as a perfect foil for the spiciness of the pilau.

chickpea & vegetable bulgur pilau

Put the onion and garlic in a large saucepan with 4 tablespoons of the stock. Cover and cook over medium heat for 5 minutes until softened.

Stir in the bulgur wheat, spices and carrots and cook for 1–2 minutes, stirring, then add the tomatoes, courgettes/zucchini, mushrooms, chickpeas and the remaining stock. Season with salt and pepper. Bring to the boil, then reduce the heat, cover and simmer for 15 minutes.

Stir the pilau, pile the spinach on top, then replace the lid and cook for a further 5 minutes. Mix the cooked spinach into the pilau and serve in warmed bowls.

1 onion, finely chopped

1 garlic clove, crushed

400 ml/1¾ cups vegetable stock

175 g/1½ cups bulgur wheat

2 teaspoons cumin seeds

1½ teaspoons ground coriander

a pinch of hot chilli powder

150 g/5½ oz. carrots, cut into 1-cm/½-inch dice

400-g/14-oz. can chopped tomatoes

275 g/9½ oz. courgettes/zucchini, diced

200 g/7 oz. mushrooms, chopped

400-g/14-oz. can chickpeas, drained and rinsed

a pinch of sea salt

200 g/7 oz. baby spinach, rinsed

freshly ground black pepper

serves 4

The cuisine of Gujerat, in north-west India, where this dish originates, is know for its interesting spice combinations, a legacy of its position on a major ancient caravan route taking spices and other goods from the East to the West. Gujerat is largely vegetarian, and rice dishes are much loved.

spicy seeded pilaf with okra & spinach

1 onion

250 g/9 oz. pattypan squash or baby courgettes/zucchini

1–1½ teaspoons hot chilli powder

½ teaspoon ground turmeric

2 tablespoons peanut oil

1 teaspoon poppy seeds, crushed

1 teaspoon cumin seeds, crushed

1 teaspoon coriander seeds, crushed

4 garlic cloves, crushed

1¼ teaspoons salt

250 g/1¼ cups white basmati rice

600 ml/2½ cups boiling vegetable stock

2 dried bay leaves (optional)

2 tablespoons coconut cream

125 g/4½ oz. okra, trimmed

125 g/4½ oz. baby spinach

125 g/4½ oz. green peas, fresh or frozen

50 g/2 oz. flaked coconut (fresh or dried)

serves 4

Slice the onion lengthways into thin segments. Toss the onion and squash in the chilli powder and turmeric. Heat the oil in a frying pan and sauté the vegetables for 1–2 minutes or until aromatic. Add the poppy, cumin and coriander seeds, the garlic and salt. Cook over moderate heat until the seeds begin to crackle and pop and become aromatic.

Stir in the rice. Sauté for another minute, stirring gently, then add the stock, bay leaves, if using, and the coconut cream. Cover and reduce the heat to simmering, then cook undisturbed for 8 minutes.

Add the okra, spinach, green peas and flaked coconut. Cover and cook for a further 4–5 minutes until the rice is tender but dry. Remove the bay leaves, stir well and serve.

This is a vegetarian take on the classic Spanish rice dish paella. It's colourful, delicious and bursting with fresh, young vegetables grown on the vine and enhanced with the subtle flavour of saffron. Perfect for summer entertaining.

paella of summer vine vegetables with almonds

Put the saffron in a bowl with 65 ml/⅓ cup hot water and set aside to infuse. Heat half of the oil in a heavy-based frying pan set over high heat and add the tomatoes. Cook for 2 minutes, shaking the pan so that the tomatoes soften and start to split. Use a slotted spoon to remove the tomatoes from the pan and set aside. Add the beans, courgettes/zucchini and peas and stir-fry over high heat for 2–3 minutes. Set aside with the tomatoes until needed.

Add the remaining oil to the pan with the garlic and rosemary and cook gently for 1 minute to flavour the oil. Add the rice to the pan and cook, stirring constantly, for 2 minutes, until the rice is shiny and opaque. Add the stock and saffron water to the pan. Stir just once or twice, then increase the heat and let the liquid reach the boil.

When the stock is rapidly boiling and little holes have formed in the rice, reduce the heat to medium and let simmer gently for about 20 minutes, until almost all the stock has been absorbed.

Scatter the cooked tomatoes, beans, courgettes/zucchini and peas over the rice, cover lightly with some foil and cook over low heat for 5 minutes so that the vegetables are just heated through. Sprinkle the almonds on top to serve.

a large pinch of saffron threads

80 ml/⅓ cup olive oil

200 g/7 oz. red or yellow cherry tomatoes

100 g/4 oz. green beans

4 baby courgettes/zucchini, halved

80 g/3 oz. freshly shelled peas

2 garlic cloves, chopped

2 fresh rosemary sprigs

320 g/1½ cups Arborio risotto rice

800 ml/3⅓ cups vegetable stock

30 g/¼ cup flaked/slivered almonds, lightly toasted

serves 4

The charm of this risotto is found in the delicate flavours and colours of spring. The vegetables are small and sweet, the herbs fresh and fragrant. Don't be tempted to skimp on the herbs here – as well as imparting intense flavour to the risotto, they add a beautiful touch of spring green.

spring risotto with herbs

about 1.5 litres/6 cups hot vegetable stock

125 g/1 stick unsalted butter

6 spring onions/scallions, finely chopped

2 garlic cloves, finely chopped, crushed

150 g/5½ oz. carrots, cubed, or a bunch of tiny new carrots, trimmed and scraped but kept whole

400 g/2 cups risotto rice, preferably carnaroli

100 g/3½ oz. asparagus spears, trimmed and cut into 2-cm/1-inch lengths

100 g/3½ oz. fine green beans, cut into 2-cm/1-inch lengths

100 g/3½ oz. fresh or frozen peas or broad beans, thawed if frozen

6 tablespoons chopped mixed fresh herbs, such as chives, dill, flat leaf parsley, mint, chervil and tarragon

50 g/⅓ cup freshly grated Parmesan-style cheese (see note on page 4), plus extra to serve

sea salt and freshly ground black pepper

serves 4

Put the stock in a saucepan and keep at a gentle simmer. Melt half the butter in a large, heavy saucepan and add the spring onions/scallions, garlic and carrots. Cook gently for 5 minutes until the onions are soft and translucent but not browned. Stir in the rice until well coated with the butter and heated through.

Begin adding the stock, a large ladle at a time, stirring gently until each ladle has almost been absorbed by the rice. The risotto should be kept at a bare simmer throughout cooking, so don't let the rice dry out – add more stock as necessary.

After 10 minutes, add the asparagus, beans and peas and continue until the vegetables are tender and the rice is tender and creamy, but the grains still firm. (This should take 15–20 minutes depending on the type of rice used – check the timings on the packet.)

Taste and season well with salt and pepper and stir in the remaining butter, the herbs and the cheese. Cover and let rest for a couple of minutes so the risotto can relax, then serve immediately with extra freshly grated cheese. You may like to add a little more hot stock to the risotto just before you serve to loosen it, but don't let it wait around too long or the rice will turn mushy.

This is a super-speedy dish. As with any recipe for a baked risotto, you are not going to get the creamy texture of one cooked by the more conventional method. That said, this recipe more than makes up for it in other ways – take simple, fresh ingredients, a few quick stirs and dinner is ready to serve.

oven-baked tomato & rosemary risotto

Preheat the oven to 200°C (400°C) Gas 6.

Put the stock in a large saucepan and set over low heat. Put the oil in a flameproof, lidded casserole dish and set over low heat. Add the onion and garlic and fry gently for 2–3 minutes until the onion has softened. Add the rice and the rosemary and cook for a further minute before adding the courgettes/zucchini. Stir for 1 minute, or until the rice becomes opaque, then add the tomatoes. Pour the hot stock into the casserole and stir well to remove any stuck-on bits and to combine all the ingredients. As soon as the liquid starts to simmer, cover with the lid and cook in the preheated oven for 30 minutes.

Stir through the butter and half of the cheese, then sprinkle the remaining cheese on top to serve.

750 ml/3 cups vegetable stock

2 tablespoons olive oil

1 onion, chopped

1 garlic clove, chopped

330 g/1½ cups short-grain white rice

2 tablespoons fresh rosemary needles

2 courgettes/zucchini, roughly chopped

2 tomatoes, chopped

3 tablespoons butter

50 g/½ cup grated Parmesan-style cheese (see note on page 4)

serves 4

This risotto needs the sweetness of the vegetables to balance the acidity from the wine. Use a good wine that you would not be ashamed to drink, and you will achieve perfect results. Use a cheap, undrinkable wine and the risotto will be inedible. Brighten it up with a scattering of emerald green chopped parsley.

red wine risotto

about 1.5 litres/6 cups hot vegetable stock

125 g/1 stick unsalted butter

1 small red onion, finely chopped

1 small carrot, finely chopped

1 small celery stick, finely chopped

500 g/2⅓ cups risotto rice

300 ml/1⅓ cups full-bodied red wine such as Barolo

125 g/1¼ cups freshly grated Parmesan-style cheese (see note on page 4)

sea salt and freshly ground black pepper

chopped fresh parsley, to serve

serves 4–6

Put the stock in a saucepan and keep at a gentle simmer. Melt half the butter in a large, heavy saucepan and add the onion, carrot and celery. Cook gently for 10–12 minutes until soft, golden and translucent but not browned. Add the rice and stir until well coated with the butter and heated through. Pour in the wine and boil hard until it has been reduced by half. This will remove the taste of raw alcohol.

Begin adding the stock, a large ladle at a time, stirring gently until each ladle has almost been absorbed by the rice. The risotto should be kept at a bare simmer throughout cooking, so don't let the rice dry out – add more stock as necessary. Continue until the rice is tender and creamy, but the grains still firm. (This should take 15–20 minutes depending on the type of rice used – check the timings on the packet.)

Taste and season well with salt and pepper and beat in the remaining butter and all the cheese. Cover and let rest for a couple of minutes so the risotto can relax, then serve immediately. You may like to add a little more hot stock to the risotto just before you serve to loosen it, but don't let it wait around too long or the rice will turn mushy. Serve sprinkled with parsley.

Butternut squash is one of the most wonderful vegetables to use in a roasted risotto as the oven-baking brings out the sweetness of the vegetable. Combined with cream, butter or cheese, the result is a creamy texture and a fantastic harmony of flavours.

roasted butternut squash risotto

Preheat the oven to 200°C (400°F) Gas 6.

Put the butternut squash on a baking sheet and sprinkle with salt and 2 tablespoons olive oil. Roast in the preheated oven for 30 minutes until tender.

Put the butter, remaining olive oil and garlic in a medium saucepan. Cook gently for 2 minutes, then add the oregano, sage and rice. Let the rice absorb the buttery juices, then stir in a ladle of the hot stock.

Wait until the stock has been absorbed, then add the wine and the rest of the stock, a ladle at a time, making sure it has been completely absorbed between each addition. Stir in the squash and lightly mash with the back of a fork, leaving some pieces whole. Stir in the lemon juice and add salt and pepper to taste.

Serve topped with a generous spoonful of mascarpone.

Note The risotto is great served with a light salad of lamb's lettuce/corn salad, thin slices of roasted courgette/zucchini and cherry tomatoes or steamed vegetables.

1 butternut squash (about 1 kg/2 lbs.), peeled, deseeded and cut into small cubes

4 tablespoons olive oil

3 tablespoons unsalted butter

2 garlic cloves, crushed

a handful of fresh oregano leaves, finely chopped

10 fresh sage leaves

275 g/1⅓ cups risotto rice, such as arborio

1.25 litres/5 cups hot vegetable stock

200 ml/¾ cup white wine

1 teaspoon lemon juice

sea salt and freshly ground black pepper

mascarpone cheese, to serve

serves 4

Any kind of fresh wild mushroom will make this taste wonderful – black trompettes de mort, deep golden girolles or musky chanterelles. However, it can be made very successfully using a mixture of cultivated mushrooms and dried reconstituted Italian porcini or French cèpes. In Italy, a wild herb called nepitella is often used when cooking wild mushrooms. It is a type of wild catnip and complements the mushrooms very well.

about 1.5 litres/6 cups hot vegetable stock

125 g/1 stick unsalted butter

1 large onion, finely chopped

2 garlic cloves, finely chopped

250 g/9 oz. mixed wild mushrooms, cleaned and coarsely chopped (or a mixture of wild and fresh, or 200 g/7 oz. cultivated mushrooms, plus 25 g/1 oz. dried porcini soaked in warm water for 20 minutes, drained and chopped)

1 tablespoon each of chopped fresh thyme and marjoram (or nepitella)

150 ml/⅔ cup dry white wine or vermouth

500 g/2½ cups risotto rice

75 g/¾ cup freshly grated Parmesan-style cheese, plus extra to serve (see note on page 4)

sea salt and freshly ground black pepper

serves 6

wild mushroom risotto

Put the stock in a saucepan and keep at a gentle simmer. Melt the butter in a large, heavy saucepan and add the onion and garlic. Cook gently for 10 minutes until soft, golden and translucent but not browned.

Stir in the mushrooms and herbs, then cook over medium heat for 3 minutes to heat through. Pour in the wine and boil hard until it has reduced and almost disappeared. This will remove the taste of raw alcohol. Stir in the rice and fry with the onion and mushrooms until dry and slightly opaque.

Begin adding the stock, a large ladle at a time, stirring until each ladle has been absorbed by the rice. Continue until the rice is tender and creamy, but the grains still firm. (This should take 15–20 minutes depending on the type of rice used – check the timings on the packet.)

Taste and season well with salt and pepper. Stir in the cheese, cover and let rest for a couple of minutes. Serve immediately with extra grated cheese.

Dill is a herb that has never been terribly fashionable, unlike its peers, rosemary and sage. It's quite a floral, grassy herb and a whiff of it conjures up springtime, which is possibly why it is so well complemented by the beans and peas in this dish. Marinating the feta lifts it from a salty, creamy cheese to something much more complex, so it's well worth it, even if it's just for 5 minutes.

couscous with feta, dill & spring beans

Put the couscous in a large bowl and pour over the boiling water. Cover with clingfilm/plastic wrap or a plate and let swell for 10 minutes.

Pour the olive oil into a mixing bowl and add the garlic, shallots, dill, chives and preserved lemon and lots of freshly ground black pepper – the coarser the better. Add the feta, turn in the oil and set aside while you cook the beans.

Bring a medium saucepan of unsalted water to the boil. Add the sugar snap peas, bring back to the boil and cook for 1 minute. Add the broad/fava beans, bring back to the boil and cook for 1 minute. Finally, add the peas and cook for 2 minutes. Drain.

Uncover the couscous, stir in the hot beans, transfer to bowls and top with the feta cheese, spooning over the flavoured oil as you go. Stir well before serving.

275 g/1¾ cups couscous

400 ml/1¾ cups boiling water

5 tablespoons extra virgin olive oil

1 garlic clove, peeled and crushed

3 shallots, peeled and thinly sliced

2 tablespoons chopped fresh dill

2 tablespoons chopped fresh chives

1 tablespoon finely chopped preserved lemon, or 1 tablespoon zest and flesh of fresh lemon, finely chopped

250 g/9 oz. vegetarian feta cheese (see note on page 4), chopped

150 g/5½ oz. sugar snap peas

150 g/5½ oz. baby broad/fava beans

150 g/5½ oz. frozen peas, defrosted

freshly ground black pepper

serves 4

Popping its head up in just about every style of cuisine, the summer-fruiting aubergine/eggplant is very versatile. It is just as much at home with tomato, basil and pecorino as with Moroccan spices, as in this dish. You will need one large aubergine/eggplant, so look for a beauty that is firm, full and heavy with shiny deep-purple skin.

moroccan-spiced couscous

65 ml/¼ cup vegetable oil

1 large aubergine/eggplant, cut into 2-cm/1-inch cubes

1 tablespoon light olive oil

280 g/1¾ cups couscous

½ teaspoon paprika

½ teaspoon chilli powder

375 ml/1½ cups vegetable stock

1 small bunch of fresh coriander/cilantro, leaves and stems, roughly chopped

50–60 g/2 oz. baby spinach

125 ml/½ cup natural/plain yogurt

lemon wedges, to serve

serves 4

Heat the vegetable oil in frying pan set over high heat and cook the aubergine/eggplant for 3–4 minutes, turning often so it is an even, golden brown. Place on kitchen paper to drain off the excess oil.

Heat the olive oil in a saucepan over medium heat. Add the couscous, paprika and chilli powder and cook for 2 minutes, stirring constantly. Add the stock and bring to the boil. Remove the pan from the heat, cover with a tight-fitting lid and let stand for 10 minutes.

Fluff the couscous with a fork, then cover and leave for a further 5 minutes. Place the couscous in a large bowl and add the aubergine/eggplant, coriander/cilantro and baby spinach and toss to combine.

Place on a serving plate with the yogurt and lemon wedges on the side to serve.

Variation Replace the aubergine/eggplant with 3 courgettes/zucchini, cut into 1-cm/½-inch wide rounds. Pan-fry them in a little light olive oil until golden on both sides. Add the courgettes/zucchini to the prepared couscous with a handful of roughly chopped fresh mint.

When buying salad leaves, keep in mind you will need about two large handfuls per person. Avoid limp looking greens. If they do wilt a little on the way home, give them a quick bath in a bowl of cold water with a pinch or two of sugar thrown in to freshen them up. The fresh spring ingredients are combined here with bulgur wheat. Simply cover with boiling water to soften and add to your favourite salad ingredients.

tabbouleh with chickpeas & spring salad

Put the bulgur wheat in a heatproof bowl and pour over 125 ml/½ cup boiling water. Stir once, cover tightly with clingfilm/plastic wrap and set aside for 8–10 minutes. Put the lemon juice and olive oil in a small bowl and whisk. Pour over the bulgur wheat and stir well with a fork, fluffing it up and separating the grains.

Put the bulgur wheat in a large bowl with the parsley, mint, dill, tomatoes, chickpeas and salad leaves. Use your hands to toss everything together. Season well with sea salt and black pepper. Transfer to a serving plate and serve with toasted Turkish bread, if you like.

90 g/½ cup fine bulgur wheat

2 tablespoons freshly squeezed lemon juice

60 ml/¼ cup extra virgin olive oil

1 small bunch of fresh flat leaf parsley, finely chopped

1 large handful of fresh mint leaves, finely chopped

2 tablespoons finely chopped fresh dill

1 small punnet of cherry tomatoes, halved

400-g/14-oz. can chickpeas, rinsed and drained

120–150 g/4–5 oz. spring salad mix

sea salt and freshly ground black pepper

toasted Turkish flat bread, to serve (optional)

serves 4

250 g/1½ cups bulgur wheat

50 g/¼ cup roasted hazelnuts, chopped

50 g/¼ cup pistachio nuts, chopped

5–6 spring onions/scallions, trimmed and thinly sliced

½ cucumber, peeled, deseeded and finely chopped

1 red ramiro pepper, halved, deseeded and finely chopped

3 ripe tomatoes, skinned and finely chopped

1 pomegranate

freshly squeezed juice of 2 lemons

½ teaspoon salt

1 teaspoon ground cumin

1 teaspoon dried chilli/hot pepper flakes

1 tablespoon pomegranate syrup or 2 teaspoons balsamic vinegar with 1 teaspoon sugar

3 tablespoons extra virgin olive oil

5 tablespoons finely chopped parsley

3 tablespoons finely chopped mint leaves

3 tablespoons finely chopped dill

sea salt and freshly ground black pepper

serves 8

This Turkish recipe is not only a great one-pot but also the perfect party salad. You can vary it depending on what you have available, substituting walnuts for hazelnuts or pistachios, for example, adding some olives or some finely snipped dried apricots or replacing the dill with fresh coriander/cilantro.

kisir

Put the bulgur wheat in a large heatproof bowl and pour over enough boiling water to just cover the grain. Leave for 15 minutes for the liquid to absorb, then pour over plenty of cold water, swirl the grain around and tip into a sieve/strainer. Squeeze the grain with your hands to extract any excess water and return the grain to the bowl.

Add the nuts, spring onions/scallions, cucumber, pepper and tomatoes (including the seeds and pulp). Halve the pomegranate and scoop out the seeds, reserving the juice and discarding the pith. Add the pomegranate seeds to the salad.

Whisk the lemon juice and reserved pomegranate juice with the salt, cumin and chilli/hot pepper flakes, whisk in the pomegranate syrup and olive oil and season with salt and pepper. Tip into the salad and mix well.

Finally, mix in the chopped herbs. Toss well together and check the seasoning, adding more salt, pepper or lemon juice to taste. Cover and set aside for at least an hour before serving for the flavours to infuse.

curries & tagines

This delicious curry is full of wonderful colours and aromas. Made with aubergine/eggplant and lentils it makes a filling dish served just as it is, but it can also be served with basmati rice alongside, if preferred.

aubergine, tomato & red lentil curry

Heat the oil in a frying pan set over high heat. When the oil is smoking hot add the aubergine/eggplant to the pan and cook for 5 minutes, turning the pieces often so that they cook evenly. At first the aubergine/eggplant will absorb the oil, but as it cooks to a dark and golden colour, the oil will start to seep out back into the pan. Remove the aubergine/eggplant from the pan at this point and not before.

Add the remaining oil, onions, garlic and ginger to the pan and cook for 5 minutes. Add the cherry tomatoes and cook for 1 minute, until they just soften and collapse, then remove them from the pan before they break up too much and set aside with the aubergine/eggplant.

Add the curry leaves and cumin to the pan and cook for a couple of minutes as the curry leaves pop and crackle. Add the chilli powder, tomato purée/paste, 480 ml/2 cups water and the lentils and simmer for 15–20 minutes, until the lentils are tender but retain some 'bite'. Stir in the aubergine/eggplant and cherry tomatoes and cook the curry for a couple of minutes just to warm through. Stir in the coriander/cilantro and serve.

3 tablespoons light olive oil

1 large aubergine/eggplant, cut into 8 pieces

1 red onion, chopped

2 garlic cloves, chopped

1 tablespoon finely chopped fresh ginger

250 g/8 oz. cherry tomatoes on the vine

6–8 curry leaves

1 teaspoon ground cumin

¼ teaspoon chilli powder

1 tablespoon tomato purée/paste

125 g/⅔ cup red split lentils

1 handful of fresh coriander/cilantro, roughly chopped

serves 4

Dhaal baht (rice and lentils) is a staple meal for millions of Indians and Nepalis. In this recipe, potatoes are added to that traditional duo, and they are particularly good for absorbing the wonderful flavours of Indian spices.

potato curry with yellow lentils

125 g/1¼ cups yellow lentils

3 tablespoons oil

½ teaspoon mustard seeds

½ teaspoon fenugreek seeds

1 teaspoon grated fresh ginger

1 teaspoon crushed garlic

1 teaspoon chilli powder

1½ teaspoons ground coriander

½ teaspoon ground turmeric

4 tomatoes, skinned and chopped

1 teaspoon salt

750 g/1½ lbs. floury potatoes, cut into 2-cm/1-inch chunks

sea salt and freshly ground black pepper

to serve

2 tablespoons chopped fresh coriander/cilantro, plus extra sprigs

½ teaspoon garam masala

basmati rice

serves 4

Wash the lentils well in several changes of water. Heat the oil in a large saucepan over low heat. Add the mustard and fenugreek seeds. When they begin to pop, stir in the ginger and garlic and fry for 30 seconds.

Add the chilli powder, ground coriander and turmeric and stir-fry for a further 30 seconds. Add the tomatoes and lentils, cover with 600 ml/ 2½ cups water, add the salt, then bring to the boil. Reduce the heat, cover and simmer for 20–30 minutes or until the lentils are just soft.

Add the potatoes and simmer over low heat for 10–15 minutes or until the potatoes are tender. Season with salt and pepper.

Serve sprinkled with chopped coriander/cilantro, garam masala and sprigs of fresh coriander/cilantro. Basmati rice makes a suitable accompaniment, if prefered.

This spinach and cheese curry uses paneer – a firm, fresh white Indian cheese. If you cannot find paneer, halloumi also works well. The other ingredients are all readily available – fresh spinach and a good-quality curry paste. Pre-made curry pastes are a great short-cut– they keep well in the refrigerator and save you from having a cupboard full of dry spices which have a short shelf life*.

spinach & cheese curry

Heat the oil in a non-stick frying pan over high heat and cook the cubes of cheese for 2–3 minutes, turning often, until golden all over. Remove the cheese to a plate and set aside until needed.

Add the butter to the pan and when sizzling hot, add the curry paste and green chillies and stir-fry for 2 minutes. Add the spinach and coriander/cilantro and cook for 3–4 minutes, until all the spinach has wilted, then stir in the cream.

Put the mixture in a food processor and process until the sauce is thick and smooth. Return to the pan, add the cheese and cook over low heat for 2–3 minutes, to warm the cheese through.

Serve the curry spooned over basmati rice with warm naan bread on the side, if you like.

*Note Not all curry pastes are vegetarian, so do make sure you check the ingredients on the jar before using.

1 tablespoon vegetable oil

250 g/9 oz. paneer or halloumi, cut into 2-cm/1-inch cubes

2 tablespoons butter

2 tablespoons mild Indian curry paste (Madras or balti)

2 large green chillies (optional), deseeded and chopped

500 g/1 lb. spinach, roughly chopped

a handful of chopped fresh coriander/cilantro, leaves and stems

125 ml/½ cup single cream

lemon wedges, to garnish

basmati rice and warm naan bread, to serve (optional)

serves 4

This recipe is based on the cuisine of Southern India, which tends to have a greater emphasis on fresh ingredients, with just one or two spices thrown in, rather than relying on dozens and dozens of dried spices. You can use halloumi instead of paneer, if prefered.

fresh tomato, pea & paneer curry

2 tablespoons vegetable oil

250 g/9 oz. paneer, cubed

1 tablespoon butter

2 onions, finely chopped

5-cm/2-inch piece of fresh ginger, grated

2 green chillies, deseeded and finely chopped

3 ripe tomatoes, roughly chopped

2 teaspoons white wine vinegar

200 g/1½ cups frozen peas

½ teaspoon garam masala

a handful of fresh coriander/cilantro leaves

sea salt and freshly ground black pepper

to serve

cooked basmati rice

naan bread

mango chutney

serves 4

Heat the oil in a frying pan set over medium heat. Add the paneer and cook for 4–5 minutes, turning often, until golden all over. Remove from the pan and set aside.

Add the butter to the pan. When it is melted and sizzling, add the onions and stir-fry until softened and lightly golden. Add the ginger and chillies to the pan and cook for 1 minute.

Add the tomatoes, vinegar and 65 ml/¼ cup water and bring to the boil. Cook for about 5 minutes, to thicken slightly. Add the peas and return the paneer to the pan. Reduce the heat and simmer for about 5 minutes, until the peas are tender.

Stir in the garam masala and season to taste with salt and pepper. Sprinkle with the coriander/cilantro leaves and serve with basmati rice and an assortment of Indian accompaniments.

When shopping for the okra, make sure that they are bright green, firm and not bruised. This dish makes a fantastic vegetarian main course. You could serve it teamed with basmati rice, dhaal and pickles, if liked.

okra masala

Heat the sunflower oil in a large, non-stick wok or frying pan over medium heat and add the curry leaves, mustard seeds and onion. Stir-fry for 3–4 minutes, then add the cumin, coriander, curry powder and turmeric. Stir-fry for 1–2 minutes, then add the garlic and okra. Stir and cook over high heat for 2–3 minutes.

Stir in the tomatoes and season well. Cover, reduce the heat to low and cook gently for 10–12 minutes, stirring occasionally, until the okra is tender.

Garnish with the grated coconut before serving with steamed basmati rice, dhaal and pickles.

2 tablespoons sunflower oil

6–8 fresh curry leaves

2 teaspoons black mustard seeds

1 onion, finely diced

2 teaspoons ground cumin

1 teaspoon ground coriander

2 teaspoons medium curry powder

1 teaspoon ground turmeric

3 garlic cloves, finely chopped

500 g/1 lb. okra, trimmed and cut diagonally into 2.5-cm/1-inch pieces

2 ripe plum tomatoes, finely chopped

3 tablespoons freshly grated coconut

serves 4

This fragrant and mild vegetable and coconut stew is called *avial* in its home town of Kerala, in the southern tip of India. Traditionally served with steamed rice pancakes, it is equally good eaten with rice or bread.

keralan vegetable stew

2 tablespoons sunflower/ safflower oil

6 shallots, thinly sliced

2 teaspoons black mustard seeds

8–10 fresh curry leaves

1 green chilli, thinly sliced

2 teaspoons finely grated fresh ginger

1 teaspoon ground turmeric

2 teaspoons ground cumin

6 black peppercorns

2 carrots, cut into thick batons

1 courgette/zucchini, cut into thick batons

200 g/7 oz. green beans

1 large potato, peeled and cut into thick batons

300 ml/1¼ cups coconut milk

100 ml/½ scant cup vegetable stock or water

freshly squeezed juice of ½ lemon

salt and freshly ground black pepper

serves 4

Heat the sunflower/safflower oil in a large, heavy-based frying pan and add the shallots. Stir and cook over medium heat for 4–5 minutes. Add the mustard seeds, curry leaves, chilli, ginger, turmeric, cumin and peppercorns and stir-fry for 1–2 minutes.

Add the carrots, courgette/zucchini, green beans and potato to the pan along with the coconut milk and stock and bring to the boil. Reduce the heat, cover and cook gently for 12–15 minutes, or until the vegetables are tender.

Season well and drizzle with the lemon juice just before serving with steamed basmati rice or bread.

This wonderfully rich pumpkin curry with creamy coconut milk and aromatic spices is a great warmer on a cold winter's day. You can use butternut squash instead of the pumpkin if you prefer.

thai red pumpkin curry

Heat the sunflower/safflower oil in a large, non-stick wok or frying pan. Add the onion, garlic and ginger and stir-fry for 3–4 minutes. Stir in the curry paste and pumpkin and stir-fry for 3–4 minutes.

Pour in the coconut milk, stock, lime leaves, lemongrass and palm sugar. Bring to the boil, then reduce the heat to low and simmer gently for 20–25 minutes, stirring occasionally, or until the pumpkin is tender.

Season well and garnish with the Thai basil leaves and shredded lime leaves just before serving.

2 tablespoons sunflower/ safflower oil

1 red onion, thinly sliced

2 garlic cloves, crushed

1 teaspoon finely grated fresh ginger

3 tablespoons Thai red curry paste

800 g/1¾ lbs. pumpkin flesh, cut into bite-sized pieces

400 ml/1⅔ cups coconut milk

150 ml/⅔ cup vegetable stock

6 kaffir lime leaves, plus extra, shredded, to garnish

3 lemongrass stalks, bruised

2 teaspoons grated palm sugar

salt and freshly ground black pepper

Thai sweet basil leaves, to garnish

serves 4

Good-quality curry pastes* are invaluable additions to your kitchen storecupboard, but give them a lift by cooking off some onion, garlic and ginger and adding fresh or dried curry leaves and a couple of large red or green chillies, split lengthways. Chickpeas are popular in India and work brilliantly here in this spicy curry. Fresh, warmed naan or roti bread makes a wonderful accompaniment.

chickpea & fresh spinach curry

1 white onion, roughly chopped

2 garlic cloves, sliced

1 teaspoon chopped fresh ginger

1 tablespoon light olive oil

2 tablespoons mild curry paste

400-g/14-oz. can chopped tomatoes

400-g/14-oz. can chickpeas, well drained and rinsed

500 g/1 lb. fresh spinach, stalks removed and leaves chopped

a handful of fresh coriander/cilantro leaves, chopped

naan or roti bread, to serve

serves 4

Put the onion, garlic and ginger in a food processor and process until finely chopped. Heat the oil in a frying pan set over high heat. Add the onion mixture and cook for 4–5 minutes, stirring often, until golden. Add the curry paste and stir-fry for just 2 minutes, until aromatic.

Stir in the tomatoes, 250 ml/1 cup cold water and the chickpeas. Bring to the boil, then reduce the heat to a medium simmer and cook, uncovered, for 10 minutes. Stir in the fresh spinach and cook just until it is wilted.

Stir in the coriander/cilantro and serve with naan or roti bread.

*Note Not all curry pastes are vegetarian, so do make sure you check the ingredients on the jar before using.

This street food of spiced chickpeas is served at little food stalls in the bazaars and markets all over India as a quick and nutritious light meal.

chickpea masala

Heat the sunflower/safflower oil in a large, heavy-based frying pan set over medium heat and add the garlic, ginger, onion and chillies. Stir-fry for 6–8 minutes, or until the onion is lightly golden. Add the cumin, chilli powder, ground coriander, yogurt and garam masala and stir-fry for 1–2 minutes.

Stir in 500 ml/2 cups water and bring to the boil. Add the curry powder, tamarind paste and chickpeas and bring back to the boil. Reduce the heat to a low simmer and cook gently for 30–40 minutes, stirring occasionally, or until the liquid has reduced, coating the chickpeas in a dark, rich sauce.

Serve in little bowls drizzled with a little whisked yogurt, garnished with chopped coriander/cilantro and chilli powder, and with lemon wedges on the side.

4 tablespoons sunflower/safflower oil

4 garlic cloves, crushed

2 teaspoons finely grated fresh ginger

1 large onion, coarsely grated

1–2 green chillies, thinly sliced

1 tablespoon ground cumin

1 teaspoon hot chilli powder, plus extra to garnish

1 tablespoon ground coriander

3 tablespoons plain yogurt, plus extra, whisked, to drizzle

2 teaspoons garam masala

2 teaspoons medium curry powder

2 teaspoons tamarind paste

2 x 400-g/14-oz. cans chickpeas, drained and rinsed

freshly chopped coriander/cilantro leaves, to garnish

lemon wedges, to serve

serves 4

Red lentils are widely used in Indian cooking to make dhaal – a lentil-based curry. They are healthy, nutritious and delicious. Serve with naan bread and top with fried curry leaves to add a splash of colour.

curried red lentils

1 onion, chopped

2 garlic cloves, chopped

2.5-cm/1-inch piece of fresh ginger, peeled and grated

40 g/4 tablespoons butter

350 g/12 oz. tomatoes, chopped

1 tablespoon curry powder

1 teaspoon ground turmeric

½ teaspoon ground cinnamon

350 g/12 oz. red split lentils

900 ml/4 cups vegetable stock

freshly squeezed juice of ½ lemon

sea salt and freshly ground black pepper

2–3 sprigs of fresh or frozen curry leaves, fried for a few seconds in 2 tablespoons butter (optional)

serves 6

Put the onion, garlic and ginger into a food processor and blend to form a fairly smooth purée. Heat the butter in a saucepan, add the purée, tomatoes and spices and fry gently for about 5 minutes.

Add the lentils, stock, lemon juice, salt and pepper, bring to the boil, cover and simmer over low heat for about 20 minutes until the lentils have thickened.

Taste and adjust the seasoning with salt and pepper, then serve topped with a few fried curry leaves, if using.

Dried red kidney beans are turned into the perfect comfort food, in this lightly spiced curry. If pushed for time, you can use good-quality organic canned red kidney beans in place of dried ones.

red kidney bean curry

Put the red kidney beans in a large saucepan, cover with cold water and let soak overnight.

Drain the soaked beans and return to the saucepan with double the amount of water. Bring to the boil, then keep boiling for 15 minutes. Reduce the heat to medium/low and simmer gently for 1 hour, or until the beans are tender. Drain, reserving the cooking liquid.

Heat the butter and sunflower/safflower oil in a large, heavy-based saucepan and add the onion, cinnamon, bay leaves, garlic and ginger and stir-fry for 4–5 minutes. Stir in the turmeric, ground coriander, cumin, garam masala and chillies.

Add the beans, tomato purée/paste and enough of the reserved cooking liquid to make a thick sauce. Bring to the boil and cook for 4–5 minutes, stirring often.

Season well, drizzle with whisked yogurt, if desired, and garnish with fresh coriander/cilantro.

250 g/1¼ cups dried red kidney beans

1 tablespoon butter

2 tablespoons sunflower/safflower oil

1 onion, finely chopped

5-cm/2-inch piece of cinnamon stick or cassia bark

2 dried bay leaves

3 garlic cloves, crushed

2 teaspoons finely grated fresh ginger

½ teaspoon ground turmeric

1 teaspoon ground coriander

2 teaspoons ground cumin

1 teaspoon garam masala

2 dried red chillies

4 tablespoons tomato purée/paste

salt and freshly ground black pepper

whisked yogurt, to drizzle (optional)

freshly chopped coriander/cilantro leaves, to serve

serves 4

Mung beans are pretty olive-coloured beans native to India and one of the most popular beans for sprouting. Once split and hulled they are yellow, have a slightly sweet flavour and become butter-soft with cooking. They are traditionally used in the Indian curry *moong dhaal*, which is flavoured with ground coriander, cumin, turmeric and hot cayenne pepper.

mung bean & vegetable curry

225 g/1 cup dried split mung beans

2 tablespoons vegetable oil

1 onion, finely chopped

2 teaspoons finely grated fresh ginger

2 garlic cloves, finely chopped

2 fresh green chillies, deseeded and finely chopped

8 curry leaves (dried or fresh)

¼ teaspoon ground turmeric

1 teaspoon ground cumin

2 carrots, sliced

400-g/14-oz. can chopped tomatoes

100 g/3½ oz. fresh spinach leaves, stalks removed and leaves chopped

leaves from a small bunch of fresh coriander/cilantro, roughly chopped

sea salt and freshly ground black pepper

naan or roti bread, to serve

serves 4

Put the mung beans in a large saucepan and add 1 litre/4 cups water. Bring to the boil, reduce the heat to a low simmer and cook for 20 minutes. Drain well and set aside.

Heat the oil in a heavy-based saucepan set over high heat. Add the onion, ginger, garlic, chillies and curry leaves. Cook for 2–3 minutes, stirring often, until the mixture is aromatic. Stir in the turmeric and cumin and cook for 1 minute more.

Add the carrot, tomatoes, mung beans and 125 ml/½ cup water and bring to the boil. Reduce the heat to a medium simmer and cook for 15 minutes, until the carrots are tender and the mung beans are soft and breaking up. Stir in the spinach and coriander/cilantro and cook for a couple of minutes, until the spinach has wilted. Season to taste with salt and pepper and serve with the Indian bread of your choice.

Varation Instead of carrots, try substituting chopped butternut squash, pumpkin, baby new potatoes or cubes of pan-fried aubergine/eggplant.

This is a very quick tagine to prepare, and you will be rewarded with sweet, caramelized tender vegetables. You can cook this recipe in the oven if you like, using the tagine base or an ovenproof dish.

tagine of butternut squash, shallots & almonds

Heat the oil and butter in a tagine or heavy-based casserole. Add the shallots and garlic and sauté, stirring, until they begin to colour. Add the sultanas/golden raisins and almonds and stir in the harissa and honey. Toss in the squash, making sure it is coated in the spicy oil. Pour in enough water to cover the base of the tagine and cover.

Cook gently for 15–20 minutes, until the shallots and squash are tender but still quite firm.

Season to taste with salt and pepper, sprinkle the coriander/cilantro leaves over the top and serve with wedges of lemon to squeeze over the dish and couscous, if liked.

3 tablespoons olive oil plus a pat of butter

12 shallots, peeled and left whole

8 garlic cloves, lightly crushed

120 g/⅔ cup sultanas/golden raisins

120 g/⅔ cup blanched almonds

1–2 teaspoons harissa paste

2 tablespoons dark, runny honey

1 medium butternut squash, halved lengthways, peeled, deseeded and sliced

sea salt and freshly ground black pepper

leaves from a small bunch of fresh coriander/cilantro, finely chopped

lemon wedges, to serve

couscous, to serve (optional)

serves 3–4

2–3 tablespoons olive oil

2 onions, halved and sliced with the grain

4 garlic cloves, chopped

a thumb-sized piece of fresh ginger, peeled and chopped

1–2 red chillies, deseeded and chopped

1 teaspoon cumin seeds

1 teaspoon paprika

3–4 good-sized potatoes, peeled and thickly sliced

2 good-sized carrots, peeled and thickly sliced

8–10 broccoli florets

600 ml/2½ cups vegetable stock

225 g/2 cups fresh or frozen peas

1 preserved lemon, thickly sliced

leaves from a bunch of fresh coriander/cilantro, coarsely chopped

sea salt and freshly ground black pepper

4–6 large tomatoes, sliced

2 tablespoons butter

crusty bread or couscous, to serve

serves 4

This vegetable tagine can be served as a side dish or on its own with couscous or flat bread to dip into it. Vegetable tagines vary with the seasons and can be prepared on the hob or in the oven. For the baked version, you need a traditional Berber tagine with a domed lid, rather than the steep conical one, or you can use an earthenware baking dish, covered with foil.

baked vegetable tagine with preserved lemon

Preheat the oven to 180°C (350°F) Gas 4.

Heat the oil in a tagine or heavy-based casserole. Add the onions and sauté until they begin to colour. Add the garlic, ginger and chillies and cook for 1–2 minutes. Stir in the cumin seeds and paprika then toss in the potatoes, carrots and broccoli. Pour in the stock, cover and place the tagine in the oven for about 20 minutes, until the potatoes, carrots and broccoli are tender but still firm and most of the liquid has reduced.

Season with salt and pepper. Toss in the peas, preserved lemon and half the coriander/cilantro. Arrange the tomato slices, overlapping each other, on top and dab them with little bits of butter. Pop the tagine back into the oven, uncovered, to brown the top of the tomatoes.

Garnish with the remaining coriander/cilantro and serve hot from the tagine with couscous or fresh crusty bread.

This is one of those dishes you'll find in Morocco at street stalls, bus stations and working men's cafes. Quick, easy and colourful, it is a great dish for lunch or a tasty snack, served with warmed flat breads.

three pepper tagine with eggs

Heat the oil in the base of a tagine, flameproof baking dish or heavy-based frying pan. Add the onions, garlic, cumin and coriander seeds and sauté, stirring, until the onions begin to soften. Toss in the peppers and olives and sauté until they begin to colour. Season well with salt and pepper.

Using your spoon, push aside the peppers to form little pockets for the eggs. Crack the eggs in the pockets and cover for 4–5 minutes until the eggs are cooked. Scatter the paprika over the top and sprinkle with the parsley. Serve immediately from the tagine or pan, with warmed flat bread on the side.

2 tablespoons olive oil or ghee

1 onion, halved lengthways and sliced

2–3 garlic cloves, chopped

1–2 teaspoons coriander seeds

1 teaspoon cumin seeds

3 bell peppers (green, red and yellow), deseeded and cut into slices

2 tablespoons green olives, pitted and finely sliced

sea salt and freshly ground black pepper

4–6 very fresh eggs

1 teaspoon paprika or dried red chilli/hot pepper flakes

leaves from a small bunch of flat leaf parsley, coarsely chopped

warmed flat breads, to serve

serves 4–6

175 g/1 cup dried butter/lima beans, soaked overnight in plenty of water

2–3 tablespoons olive oil plus a pat of butter

4 garlic cloves, halved and crushed

2 red onions, halved lengthways, cut in half crossways, and sliced with the grain

1–2 red or green chillies, deseeded and thinly sliced

1–2 teaspoons coriander seeds, crushed

2-cm/1-inch piece of fresh ginger, peeled and finely shredded or chopped

a pinch of saffron threads

16–20 cherry tomatoes

1–2 teaspoons sugar

1–2 teaspoons dried thyme

2–3 tablespoons black olives, pitted

freshly squeezed juice of 1 lemon

sea salt and freshly ground black pepper

leaves from a small bunch of flat leaf parsley, coarsely chopped

crusty bread and plain yogurt, to serve (optional)

serves 4–6

As butter/lima beans are so meaty, this tagine makes a substantial main dish, although it is great served with fresh crusty bread to mop up the delicious juices. Bean dishes like this vary from region to region in Morocco, sometimes spiked with chillies.

tagine of beans, cherry tomatoes & olives

Drain and rinse the soaked beans. Put them in a deep saucepan with plenty of water and bring to the boil. Boil for about 5 minutes, then reduce the heat and simmer gently for about 1 hour, or until the beans are tender but not mushy. Drain and refresh under cold running water.

Heat the olive oil and butter in a tagine or heavy-based casserole. Add the garlic, onions and chillies and sauté, stirring, until they soften. Add the coriander seeds, ginger and saffron. Cover and cook gently for 4–5 minutes. Toss in the tomatoes with the sugar and thyme, cover with the lid, and cook until the skin on the tomatoes begins to crinkle.

Toss in the beans and olives, pour over the lemon juice and season to taste with salt and pepper. Cover and cook gently for about 5 minutes, until the beans and olives are heated through. Sprinkle with the flat leaf parsley and serve with crusty bread and a dollop of thick, creamy plain yogurt, if liked.

Chickpeas provide the nourishing content of this rustic, country-style dish. To avoid lengthy preparation, use canned chickpeas. For simple accompaniments, offer plain yogurt and fresh crusty bread.

spicy carrot & chickpea tagine with turmeric

Heat the oil in a tagine or heavy-based casserole. Add the onion and garlic and sauté, stirring, until soft. Add the turmeric, cumin seeds, cinnamon, cayenne pepper, black pepper, honey and carrots. Pour in enough water to cover the base of the tagine and cover. Cook gently for about 10–15 minutes.

Toss in the chickpeas, check that there is still enough liquid at the base of the tagine, adding a little more water if necessary. Cover with the lid, and cook gently for 5–10 minutes until all the vegetables are tender.

Season with salt, sprinkle the rosewater and coriander/cilantro leaves over the top and arrange the lemon wedges on the side. Serve with crusty bread and a dollop of thick, creamy plain yogurt, if liked.

3–4 tablespoons olive oil

1 onion, finely chopped

3–4 garlic cloves, finely chopped

2 teaspoons ground turmeric

1–2 teaspoons cumin seeds

1 teaspoon ground cinnamon

½ teaspoon cayenne pepper

½ teaspoon ground black pepper

1 tablespoon dark, runny honey

3–4 medium carrots, sliced on the diagonal

2 x 400-g/14-oz. cans chickpeas, rinsed and drained

sea salt

1–2 tablespoons rosewater

leaves from a bunch of fresh coriander/cilantro, finely chopped

lemon wedges, to serve

crusty bread and plain yogurt, to serve (optional)

serves 4

index

recipe credits

Nadia Arumugam
Buddha's delight
Green vegetables with miso
& sake
Spiced mixed vegetables with
cumin & fennel seeds
Udon noodles with tofu &
shiitake mushrooms

Ghillie Başan
Baked vegetable tagine with
preserved lemon
Chickpea salad with onions
& paprika
Country salad with peppers
& chillies
Moroccan ratatouille with dates
Spicy carrot & chickpea tagine
with turmeric
Tagine of beans, cherry
tomatoes & olives
Tagine of butternut squash,
shallots & almonds
Three pepper tagine with eggs

Fiona Beckett
Chard, onion & cheese gratin
Kisir

Celia Brooks Brown
Pad thai

Maxine Clark
Mediterranean vegetables
baked with fontina
Parmigiana di melanzane
Potato & mushroom gratin
Potatoes dauphinoise
Red wine risotto
Spring risotto with herbs
Tuscan bread & summer
vegetable salad
Wild mushroom risotto

Ross Dobson
Asparagus tagliatelle
Aubergine, tomato & red lentil
curry
Baked spinach mornay
Barley & autumn vegetable
soup
Chickpea & fresh spinach curry
Chickpea, tomato & green bean
minestrone
Creamy curried parsnip & butter
bean soup
Fresh tomato, pea & paneer
curry
Garlic & chilli rice soup with
spring greens
Greek salad with butter beans
Moroccan-spiced couscous

Mung bean & vegetable curry
Napolitana lentil stew
Orange vegetable pilau
Oven-baked tomato & rosemary
risotto
Paella of summer vine
vegetables with almonds
Pasta e fagioli
Peppery watercress & pea soup
with blue cheese
Roasted early autumn
vegetables with chickpeas
Slow-cooked onion & cider soup
with cheese toasts
Smoky hotpot of great northern
beans
Spaghetti with broccoli, walnuts
& ricotta
Spaghetti with butternut squash
& sage
Spiced cauliflower with red
pepper & peas
Spicy pinto bean soup with
shredded lettuce & sour
cream
Spinach & cheese curry
Tabbouleh with chickpeas &
spring salad
Tenderstem broccoli & potato
frittata

Clare Ferguson
Spicy seeded pilaf with okra
& spinach

Silvana Franco
Roasted vegetable pasta
Three-cheese baked penne

Manisha Gambhir Harkins
Vegetable stir-fry with szechuan
peppercorns

Tonia George
Chunky puy lentil & vegetable
soup
Couscous with feta, dill & spring
beans
Lentil, spinach & cumin soup
Linguine with lemon, basil &
cream
Stir-fried asparagus, tofu &
peppers with lemongrass,
lime leaves & honey
Tagliatelle with peas & goats'
cheese pesto
Tortilla with potatoes, chillies &
roasted pimentos
Winter-spiced salad with pears,
honeyed pecans & ricotta
Zesty summer broth

Brian Glover
Roasted squash & tomato soup
with cumin & rosemary

Amanda Grant
Stir-fry with vegetables & ginger

Rachael Anne Hill
Chickpea & vegetable bulgur
pilau
Mustardy mushroom stroganoff

Annie Nichols
Potato curry with yellow lentils

Jane Noraika
Buckwheat noodles in miso
ginger broth
Calabrian-style potatoes &
peppers
Roasted butternut squash
risotto
Roasted vegetable dauphinois
Trottole pasta salad with
peppers & garlic

Elsa Petersen-Schepelern
Indian potato salad
Pattypan & snake beans in spicy
coconut milk

Louise Pickford
Curried red lentils
Frittata with fresh herbs &
ricotta
Penne with blue cheese, pecan
& mascarpone sauce
Quick vegetarian mole
Stir-fried tofu with chilli coconut
sauce

Rena Salaman
Okra with dried limes

Jennie Shapter
Caramelized onion & blue
cheese omelette
Chickpea tortilla
Feta cheese & tomato open
omelette
Minted courgette frittata
Spicy spaghetti frittata
Sun-dried tomato frittata

Fiona Smith
Iceberg, blue cheese & date
salad with saffron & walnut
dressing

Linda Tubby
Baked rice with garlic
Vegetable sauté

Sunil Vijayakar
Chickpea masala
Keralan vegetable stew
Okra masala
Red kidney bean curry
Thai red pumpkin curry

Fran Warde
Field mushroom tortilla
Noodle mountain
Stuffed peppers

Laura Washburn
Courgette gratin with fresh
herbs & goats' cheese
Greek summer vegetable stew
with lemon & olives
Orzo pilaf
Ratatouille
Root vegetable gratin
Sweet potato, spinach &
chickpea stew with coconut
Wild mushroom & potato ragout
with leek

photography credits

Caroline Arber
Pages 46c, 52

Henry Bourne
Page 20

Martin Brigdale
Pages 2–3, 6ac, 6cr, 38, 61, 83,
116r, 122, 124, 125, 129, 130,
136, 137, 141, 144l, 145, 146,
162, 163, 168, 171, 175, 183,
187, 191, 200r, 226, 229, 230,
233, 234

Peter Cassidy
Pages 1, 6c, 8–9, 17, 21, 25, 30,
34, 41, 42, 54, 64, 73, 90l, 93,
95, 100, 105, 131, 133, 134,
143, 144r, 147, 149, 150, 151,
153, 156, 173, 178, 199, 201,
217, 220, 221, 225, 227

Tara Fisher
Pages 6ar, 46l, 46r, 47, 48, 55,
56, 59, 60, 63, 90r, 112, 185

Jonathan Gregson
Pages 6cl, 51, 81

Jeremy Hopley
Pages 103, 179

Caroline Hughes
Page 39

Richard Jung
Pages 6al, 6bl, 6bc, 14, 22, 26,
27, 29, 49, 67, 68l, 69, 77, 85,
86, 87, 90c, 91, 96, 104, 107,
108, 116l, 117, 121, 138, 142,
157, 158, 166, 170l, 170r, 172,
180, 184, 195, 196, 200l, 202,
206, 215, 235

William Lingwood
Pages 4–5, 70, 74, 99, 115, 118,
161, 169, 188, 203

Diana Miller
Pages 16, 32, 33, 37, 71, 76

David Munns
Pages 68r, 89

Noel Murphy
Pages 144c, 165

Peter Myers
Page 205

Gloria Nicol
Page 44

William Reavell
Pages 10, 11, 45, 66, 68c, 82,
98, 110, 111, 116c, 119, 126,
170c, 176, 190, 192, 197

Yuki Sugiura
Pages 13, 18

Debi Treloar
Pages 92, 154

Ian Wallace
Page 78

Kate Whitaker
Pages 6br, 200c, 208, 209, 210,
213, 214, 218, 222